Table of Contents

ABBREVIATIONS

ACT	Artemisinin-based combination therapy
AGA	AngloGold Ashanti Mining Company
AMFm	Affordable Medicines Facility - malaria
ANC	Antenatal care
BCC	Behavior change communication
CDC	Centers for Disease Control and Prevention
CHPS	Community-based Health Planning and Services
CLU	Clinical laboratory unit
CSO	Civil society organization
DfID	Department for International Development, UK
DHIMS	District Health Information Management System
DHS	Demographic and Health Survey
EPI	Expanded Program on Immunization
FDA	Food and Drug Authority
FELTP	Field Epidemiologic and Laboratory Training Program
FY	Fiscal year
G2G	Government-to-Government
GHI	Global Health Initiative
GHS	Ghana Health Service
Global Fund	Global Fund to Fight AIDS, Tuberculosis and Malaria
GOG	Government of Ghana
HCW	Health care worker
HIV/AIDS	Human immunodeficiency Virus/Acquired Immune Deficiency Syndrome
ICCM	Integrated community case management
IPTp	Intermittent preventive treatment of pregnant women
IRS	Indoor residual spraying
ITN	Insecticide-treated net
LCS	Licensed chemical sellers
LLIN	Long-lasting insecticide-treated net
M&E	Monitoring and evaluation
MCH	Maternal and child health
MICS	Multiple Indicator Cluster Survey
MIP	Malaria in pregnancy
MOH	Ministry of Health
MOP	Malaria Operational Plan
NHIA	National Health Insurance Agency
NHIS	National Health Insurance Scheme
NGO	Non-governmental organization
NMCP	National Malaria Control Program
OTSS	Outreach Training and Supportive Supervision
PMI	President's Malaria Initiative
RDT	Rapid diagnostic test
SHEP	School Health Education Program

RHIS	Routine health information systems
SP	Sulfadoxine-pyremethamine
TES	Therapeutic efficacy surveillance
UNICEF	United Nations Children's Fund
USG	United States Government
USAID	United States Agency for International Development
WHO	World Health Organization

EXECUTIVE SUMMARY

Malaria prevention and control is a major foreign assistance objective of the U.S. Government (USG). In May 2009, President Barack Obama announced the Global Health Initiative (GHI), a comprehensive effort to reduce the burden of disease and promote healthy communities and families around the world. Through the GHI, the United States will help partner countries improve health outcomes, with a particular focus on improving the health of women, newborns, and children. The President's Malaria Initiative (PMI) is a core component of the GHI.

PMI was launched in June 2005 as a 5-year, $1.2 billion initiative to rapidly scale up malaria prevention and treatment interventions and reduce malaria-related mortality by 50% in 15 high-burden countries in sub-Saharan Africa. With the passage of the 2008 Lantos-Hyde Act, funding for PMI was extended and, as part of the GHI, the goal of PMI was adjusted to reduce malaria-related mortality by 70% in the original 15 countries by the end of 2015. This will be achieved by continuing to scale up coverage of the most vulnerable groups — children under five years of age and pregnant women — with proven preventive and therapeutic interventions, including artemisinin-based combination therapies (ACTs), insecticide-treated nets (ITNs), intermittent preventive treatment of pregnant women (IPTp), and indoor residual spraying (IRS).

Ghana became a PMI country in December 2007. Other donor partners include the Global Fund to fight AIDS, Tuberculosis and Malaria (Global Fund), which has provided an estimated $145 million towards malaria control since 2003 and the Department for International Development DfID whose 5-year, $16 million begins in 2013.

Malaria is endemic and perennial in all parts of the country, with seasonal variations that are more pronounced in the north. Ghana's entire population of 24.2 million (2010 Census) is at risk of malaria infection, but children under five years of age and pregnant women are at higher risk of severe illness due to lowered immunity. Transmission is markedly less intense in large urban centers as compared to rural areas.

The PMI/Ghana FY 2014 Malaria Operational Plan (MOP) was developed in collaboration with the Government of Ghana (GOG), National Malaria Control Program (NMCP), and other development partners; analyzed malaria control data and trends; and reviewed lessons learned over four years of PMI implementation. The 2011 Multiple Indicator Cluster Survey (MICS) provided data on point prevalence of parasitemia as well as information on trends in malaria control interventions. The FY 2014 planned budget is $27 million.

ITNs

Beginning in late 2012, the long-lasting insecticide-treated net (LLIN) strategy shifted from mass campaigns to support for routine LLINs distribution, focusing on antenatal care (ANC) clinics and Expanded Program on Immunization (EPI) clinics as well as school-based distributions. With FY 2014 funding, PMI plans to continue to work with the Global Fund to sustain universal coverage through the routine distribution strategy. PMI plans to procure and distribute 300,000 LLINs; support the GOG to implement the routine LLIN distribution system; and promote LLIN use.

IRS

The PMI technical support for IRS in Ghana and related entomological monitoring continues to be an important component in malaria control. Epidemiological data from the PMI IRS spray districts have raised questions on the optimal efficacy and deployment of IRS in Ghana. As a result, PMI has supported several enhanced monitoring and evaluation (M&E) activities in the spray districts to better identify the circumstances under which IRS has its greatest impact. In addition, PMI is supporting an IRS scoping exercise to identify other potential areas to optimally deploy IRS. With the results from these activities expected in late 2013, a revised decision on the 2014 and 2015 spray season will be made by January 2014. Until that point, PMI plans to continue the FY 2013 activities in the Northern region: spraying 4 districts with organophosphates, employing enhanced information, education and communication and behavior change communication (BCC) efforts to increase ITN usage, and maintaining intensive epidemiologic and entomologic monitoring.

Malaria in Pregnancy

The PMI strategy for malaria in pregnancy (MIP) is to continue to work to provide in-service training, pre-service training and supportive supervision to maintain the knowledge, skills and practices of IPTp among healthcare workers at ANC clinics and expand IPTp capacity at peripheral healthcare facilities and services. PMI will emphasize support for ANC and IPTp in regions where the IPTp rates are lagging. Additionally, PMI will encourage malaria prevention during pregnancy through vector control by supporting the routine distribution of LLINs to pregnant women during their first ANC visit.

Case Management

With FY 2014 funding, PMI will significantly increase support for malaria case management. PMI will procure approximately 5.5 million rapid diagnostic tests (RDTs) and 4.5 million treatments of pediatric ACTs. Support from PMI will improve the knowledge, skills, and practices of healthcare workers who have received malaria case management training in the past and expand malaria case management capacity to Community-based Health Planning and Services (CHPS) zones and peripheral healthcare facilities. The PMI strategy includes funding to support private sector case management approaches through National Health Insurance Agency (NHIA) accredited pharmacy and licensed chemical sellers (LCS). PMI activities will strengthen the connections between these private sector health services providers with the Ghana Health Services (GHS) and support activities to address incentives for malaria case management compliance.

M&E

The FY 2014 PMI plan supports the NMCP to strengthen routine health information systems for malaria M&E through continued training and supportive supervision of district and regional data management staff. Implementation of the revised District Health Information Management System (DHIMS2) is fairly new; PMI will support an evaluation of the system to identify strengths, weaknesses, opportunities and threats based upon stakeholder input, a desk review and field based data collection. In line with the NMCP and PMI strategies, FY 2014 support will continue monitoring nationwide insecticide resistance and efficacy of antimalarial drugs for vector control.

I. STRATEGY

INTRODUCTION

GLOBAL HEALTH INITIATIVE AND PRESIDENT'S MALARIA INITIATIVE

Malaria prevention and control is a major foreign assistance objective of the U.S. Government (USG). In May 2009, President Barack Obama announced the Global Health Initiative (GHI), a comprehensive effort to reduce the burden of disease and promote healthy communities and families around the world. Through the GHI, the United States will help partner countries improve health outcomes, with a particular focus on improving the health of women, newborns and children. The GHI is a global commitment to invest in healthy and productive lives, building upon and expanding the USG's successes in addressing specific diseases and issues.

The President's Malaria Initiative (PMI) is a core component of the GHI. PMI was launched in June 2005 as a 5-year, $1.2 billion initiative to rapidly scale up malaria prevention and treatment interventions and reduce malaria-related mortality by 50% in 15 high-burden countries in sub-Saharan Africa. With passage of the 2008 Lantos-Hyde Act, funding for PMI was extended and, as part of the GHI, the goal of the PMI has been adjusted to reduce malaria-related mortality by 70% in the original 15 countries by the end of 2015. This will be achieved by continuing to scale up coverage of the most vulnerable groups - children under five years of age and pregnant women - with proven preventive and therapeutic interventions, including artemisinin-based combination therapies (ACTs), insecticide-treated nets (ITNs), intermittent preventive treatment of pregnant women (IPTp), and indoor residual spraying (IRS).

Ghana was selected as a PMI country in fiscal year (FY) 2007. The Ghana Health Services (GHS) began large-scale implementation of ACTs and IPTp in 2005-06 with Global Fund to fight AIDS, Tuberculosis and Malaria (Global Fund) (Round 4) support, and has progressed rapidly with the scale up of interventions with support from PMI and other partners. The NMCP is leading activities to scale up and sustain universal coverage of long-lasting insecticide-treated net (LLIN) ownership and use. The national strategy also calls for scale up of IRS to cover one third of Ghana's districts.

This FY 2014 Malaria Operational Plan (MOP) presents a detailed annual implementation plan for Ghana, based on the PMI Strategy and the National Malaria Control Program's (NMCP's) 7-Year Strategy. The MOP was developed in consultation with the NMCP and with the participation of national and international partners, including the Global Fund. This document briefly reviews the current status of malaria control policies and interventions in Ghana, describes progress to date, identifies challenges and unmet needs if the targets of the NMCP and PMI are to be achieved, and provides a description of planned FY 2014 activities.

MALARIA SITUATION IN GHANA

Malaria is endemic and perennial in all parts of Ghana, with seasonal variations that are more pronounced in the north. Ghana's entire population of 24.2 million is at risk of malaria infection, but children under five years of age and pregnant women are at higher risk of severe illness due to lowered immunity. According to GHS health facility data, malaria is the number one cause of morbidity and mortality in children under five years of age, currently accounting for 33% of hospital deaths in children under five years and about 38% of all outpatient illnesses and 36% of all admissions. Between 3.1 and 3.5 million annual cases of clinical malaria are reported in public health facilities, of which 900,000 cases are in children under five years and 3,000-4,000 result in inpatient deaths.

The World Health Organization (WHO) recently estimated total malaria-attributable child deaths at 14,000 per year in Ghana (WHO World Malaria Report 2008). Estimates for later years are not available. The verbal autopsy component of the 2008 Demographic and Health Survey (DHS) household survey found that roughly half of the deaths in children under-five occurred at home – which helps to explain the discrepancy between facility and total deaths. The high proportion of deaths occurring at home highlights the importance of improving access to treatment in the high burden areas of the country. Although malaria is commonly over-diagnosed in children who present to health facilities (particularly in urban areas), it may be undertreated in rural areas, taking into consideration the constraints to health care access.

The malaria transmission season ranges from approximately 6-7 months in the northernmost part of the country (May-October) up to 10-11 months in the forest zone. Peak levels of malaria infection and malaria-associated anemia in the population persist for two to three months into the dry season.

Plasmodium falciparum accounts for 85-90% of all infections. *Plasmodium malariae (<10%)* is also found and more rarely *P. ovale* (0.15%). The major vectors are *Anopheles gambiae* species complex and *An. funestus*. These species generally bite late in the night, are indoor resting, and are most common in the rural and peri-urban areas. Outdoor biting is common in the northern savannah (>50% outdoor biting pre-IRS was documented at several monitoring sites in Northern Region). *Anopheles melas* is found in the mangrove swamps of the southwest and *An. arabiensis* in savannah areas of northern Ghana.

Ghana can be stratified roughly into three malaria epidemiologic zones: the northern savannah; the tropical rainforest; and the coastal savannah/mangrove swamps. Although the boundaries of these zones have not been defined precisely, the demarcations used by the Ghana Statistical Service in its periodic living standards surveys since 1998 provide a close approximation. (See Figure 2) Malaria surveillance is not adequate to permit a robust subnational stratification. However, the *Ghana Multiple Indicator Cluster Survey (MICS) with Malaria Biomarker Survey*, conducted from mid-September to mid-December 2011 (the late rainy season), provides a rough snapshot of regional and zonal differences in parasitemia malaria prevalence (Figures 1 and 2).

Ghana is urbanizing rapidly, with the 2010 census demonstrating that over 50% of the population now live in urban areas. Published research and the 2011 MICS/Malaria Indicator Survey show that malaria transmission tends to be significantly less intense in large urban centers -- as documented in the PMI-supported Ghana Urban Malaria Study released in April 2013 (explained further in the monitoring and evaluation (M&E) section). Parasitemia rates among children under five in the three large cities were found to be significantly lower than the level in rural areas in the same ecologic zone. The proportion of children with a recent fever who tested positive for malaria was 80.2% in rural areas, but just 6.6% in Accra and Kumasi.

Figure 1. Malaria Prevalence in Children 6-59m, by Region. Source: 2011 MICS.

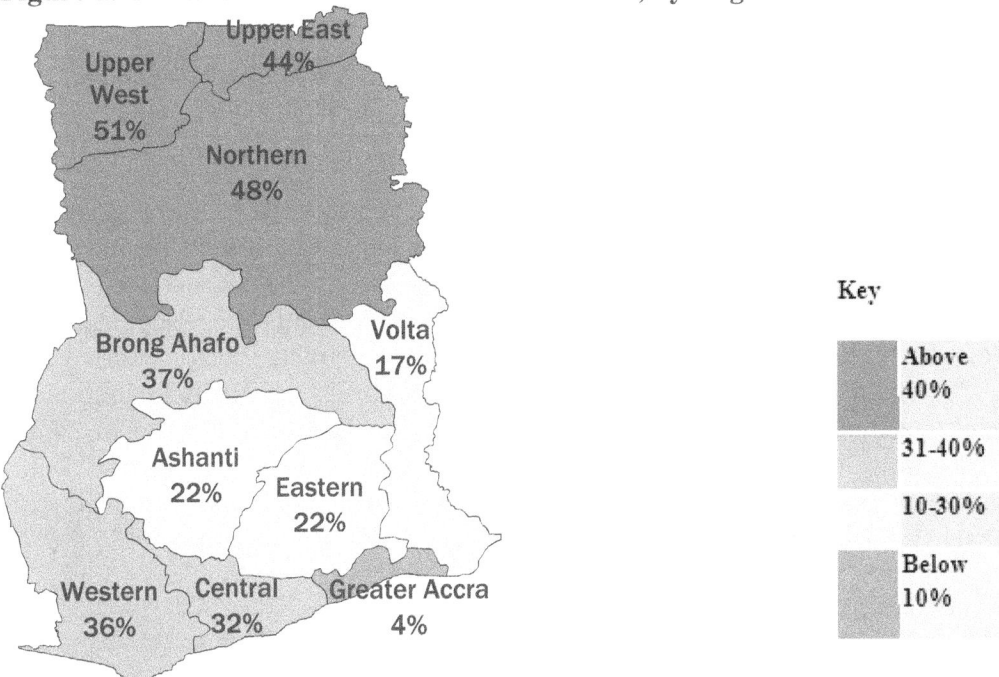

Figure 2. Malaria Prevalence in Children 6-59m, by Ecologic Zones. Source: 2011 MICS.

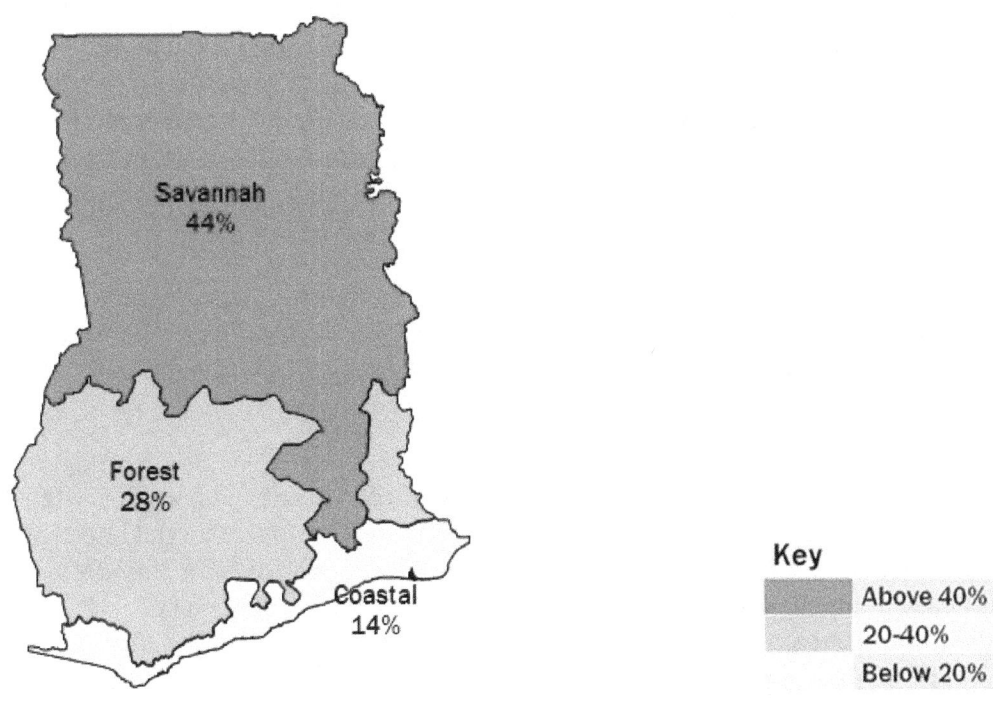

HEALTH SYSTEM DELIVERY STRUCTURE AND MINISTRY OF HEALTH ORGANIZATION

The Ministry of Health (MOH) exercises oversight and control over policy formulation and M&E of progress in achieving targets. The GHS is responsible for delivery of public health and clinical services, in parallel with the three teaching hospitals in Accra, Kumasi, and Tamale. The National Health Insurance Scheme (NHIS), implemented since 2006, represents a major development in health system financing and has increased attendance at health facilities.

The GHS operates at four levels: national, regional, district, and sub-district. Policies and major aspects of program design are developed at the national level by the central leadership and programs, such as the NMCP, while implementation and management of health services is primarily the responsibility of the decentralized Health Management Teams at the regional, district, and sub-district levels. The ratio of 1.1 skilled healthcare workers (doctors, nurses, and midwives) per 1,000 population falls short of the WHO minimum of 2.3 per 1,000 population needed by countries to achieve the millennium development goals. There are 343 hospitals, 760 health centers, 1,200 clinics in the country, and 379 private maternity homes. Of these, 83% are in the public sector and 9% are faith-based institutions, most of which are closely integrated with the GHS. The remaining 8% of facilities are in the private sector and located primarily in the larger cities.

The GHS has rolled out an updated electronic District Health Information Management System (DHIMS2). The system was scaled up in early 2012, with PMI supporting improved malaria data quality. By midyear, the new DHIMS2 system was providing monthly reports that met benchmarks for completion and timeliness resulting in the phase out of NMCP's parallel reporting system.

The penetration of the GHS services at the community level is variable. The GHS is expanding the innovative Community-Based Health Planning and Services (CHPS) program, which provides access to community health nurses in communities of at least 6,000 people. The CHPS program has grown from 300 to 1,654 CHPS zones between 2009 and 2012. A CHPS zone refers to the base of operation for a community health nurse and consists of a two-room facility with equipment for basic curative and preventive care. In many rural areas, networks of government-trained community health volunteers promote public health services.

With government decentralization of services in Ghana, regional and district level malaria control activities are managed and implemented by the Malaria Focal Persons and/or the Disease Control Officers who report to the Regional and District Health Management Teams.

NATIONAL MALARIA CONTROL PLAN & STRATEGY

In the past two decades, Ghana's strategies for malaria control have evolved and been consistent in improving control methods, increasing resources, and adopting revised international technical standards. In 2002-04, Ghana adopted ACTs as the first-line antimalarial drugs. In 2003-04, IPTp using sulfadoxine-pyrimethamine (SP) was adopted as the national policy, to be implemented by the Reproductive Health Division in collaboration with the NMCP. From 2003, international support for malaria control increased sharply, as Ghana benefitted from a succession of Global Fund grants, the launch of PMI in 2007, and significant additional support from Department for International Development, UK (DfID), United Nations Children's Fund (UNICEF), Japanese Government, the World Bank, China and Cuba. Beginning in 2005, IRS was implemented on a district-wide scale by the AngloGold Ashanti (AGA) mining company in Obuasi, Ashanti Region.

The availability of unprecedented external resources encouraged the NMCP to pursue aggressive scale up of proven malaria control methods, as captured in the *National Malaria Control Strategy 2008-2015.* The plan calls for a 75% reduction in malaria morbidity and mortality by the year 2015, using the 2006 MICS as the baseline. The key targets of the national strategy include:

1. **Universal coverage with ITNs.** Targets: One ITN available per two persons by 2013; 100% household ownership by 2015; and 85% of children under five years of age and pregnant women and 80% of the general population, sleeping under an ITN by 2015.
2. **Rapid scale-up of IRS** to cover one third of the country. Target: 90% of all structures in targeted districts are sprayed.
3. **Universal coverage of pregnant women with IPTp** using SP. Target: 100% of pregnant women receiving at least two doses of IPTp by 2015.
4. **Early diagnosis of malaria using microscopy or rapid diagnostic test (RDT).** Target: originally allowed for empiric diagnosis in children under 5 years of age, but amended in 2009 to aim for universal testing as soon as practicable.
5. **Prompt and effective treatment with ACTs**. Target: 90% of patients with uncomplicated malaria will be correctly treated using ACTs at public and private facilities by 2015.

The plan also calls for strengthening M&E systems and research; strengthening health systems at all levels; and creating and sustaining partnerships for malaria control.

In 2009, a revised *Integrated Vector Control Strategy* was released and a national Malaria Vector Control Oversight Committee was established with PMI support. This committee's mandate is to ensure safe and effective implementation and management of malaria vector control operations, in accordance with WHO guidelines and local Environmental Protection Agency pesticides regulation requirements. The NMCP *Malaria Control Communications Strategy* was released in May 2010.

Since 2008, the MOH has sponsored the Cuban Labiofam company to conduct larviciding, beginning with a pilot in central Accra and expanding to central urban districts of Kumasi, and Sunyani. The program has reported to Malaria Vector Control Oversight Committee that it regularly monitors and treats more than 1,120 anopheline breeding sites.

In light of the marked inter-regional and urban/rural difference in malaria burden, the NMCP, in collaboration with major malaria partners - the Global Fund, DfID, and PMI - are moving away from the de facto "one size fits all" approach to programming malaria control interventions which characterized the past decade. Every effort will be made to tailor malaria control interventions and case management based on the unique needs of different localities.

The national strategy is currently undergoing a routine mid-course review, supported by Roll Back Malaria and partners, which will be captured in the forthcoming report of the National Malaria Program Review. At the time of the MOP exercise in May 2013, the National Malaria Program Review had completed its desk review and field work phases, and had issued a preliminary debrief. The PMI Ghana team has provided comments and input into the report. The aide memoire and report were pending at the time of writing.

INTEGRATION, COLLABORATION, AND COORDINATION

Funding

The PMI program in Ghana has traditionally been designed to provide technical assistance and fill funding and commodity gaps in support of the country's malaria control program. Given the pivotal role played by the Global Fund grants in Ghana, PMI is working with the NMCP and coordinating closely with the Global Fund Ghana portfolio manager to plan for the most effective use of resources available. During the period overlapping the FY14 MOP, the Global Fund will be supporting two active malaria grants—one to AGA as Principal Recipient and the other to the NMCP/MOH.

AGA is currently implementing the second year of an expanded IRS program using Global Fund grant (Round 8) financing. Phase 2 of this grant, which was close to approval as of June 2013, is expected to provide $90 million in funding to implement IRS in 35 target districts through February 2015. The Phase 2 proposal emphasizes an evidenced-based approach to IRS scale up and includes operations research on the impact of combining IRS with ITNs; further scale up of the sentinel site surveillance system in IRS areas; and entomologic monitoring.

The NMCP continues to implement case management, IPTp, and ITN distribution with major support from the Global Fund -- currently under a Single Stream Financing arrangement, which consolidated several earlier grants including (Round 4/Rolling Continuous Channel, Round 8, and Affordable Medicines Facility - malaria (AMFm). As of June 2013, the NMCP was in the process of negotiating the Phase 2 proposal and budget for this grant. The Phase 2 grant will amount to approximately $55 million in new financing, plus an estimated $22 million in Phase I pipeline, and will run through February 2015. Due to procurement delays in implementing Phase 1 of its grants, the NMCP grant's score had dropped to a B2 rating (since improved to B1), which means that the country would only receive a reduced percentage of its original funding application.

The proposal for Phase 2 grant will focus heavily on sustaining universal coverage of ITNs, scale up of diagnostics and continued support for treatment in the public and private sectors. New elements include a pilot of seasonal chemoprevention in Upper East Region, at the behest of WHO, and the establishment of health facility sentinel sites for monitoring malaria case burden in all regions (protocols yet to be determined). The Phase 2 proposal also includes support for training, supervision, and data quality audits to improve data quality in the DHIMS.

DfID expects to provide approximately £10 million (approximately $16 million) over five years beginning in 2013 to support malaria control in Ghana, including support for LLINs, malaria diagnostics, and malaria case management. PMI and DfID are coordinating closely on future program planning.

The USG is well represented and engaged in oversight bodies in Ghana such as the Health Sector Working Group organized by the MOH, the Country Coordination Mechanism for the Global Fund, and the semi-annual Health Summits that draw participants from all over the country to review and plan national health interventions. In addition, the USG coordinates with malaria control stakeholders through multiple committees organized under the NMCP, including the Malaria Vector Control Oversight Committee, the LLIN Coordinating Committee, and the National Malaria Communications Committee. Regrettably, the country's Roll Back Malaria Coordinating Committee became defunct in 2008 and has yet to be revived by the MOH in spite of advocacy by WHO and PMI. The National Malaria Program Review has highlighted this deficiency, creating the expectation that this essential national body will be reconstituted by the end of 2013.

Private Sector

Ghana has a large and rapidly growing private sector and in the past decade has witnessed tremendous growth in private sector engagement in malaria control. This has encompassed corporate social responsibility programs (e.g. AGA/Global Fund, oil companies), work place health care promotion efforts (e.g. mines and plantations), and marketing of malaria medications and preventative services (e.g. pharmaceutical manufacturers, sanitation companies, and larviciding). As expected, not all private sector engagement has been aligned with NMCP policy or international public health interests, for example—the distribution of substandard medications, the confusion of garbage control with anopheles control, and the aggressive marketing of new health and diagnostic technology.

PMI continues to work to improve malaria diagnostics, treatment, and referrals in the private sector, specifically community businesses, such as pharmacies and licensed chemical sellers (LCS). PMI will coordinate with the NMCP, GHS, National Drugs Program, Pharmacy Council, Government of Ghana (GOG) researchers, pharmacy associations, and other stakeholders to introduce RDT diagnosis and scale up appropriate case management or referral of clients at LCS and pharmacies.

PMI also works with larger private sector companies involved in malaria control in Ghana, as well. AGA, as part of its corporate social responsibility program, established a malaria control program in Obuasi District in 2005 and has been implementing IRS together with targeted larviciding and other interventions. In October 2009, Ghana secured a $138 million Global Fund Round 8 grant for scale up of IRS to at least 35 districts by 2015. AngloGold Ashanti Malaria Control, which is a foundation set up by AGA, was chosen to be the grant's Principal Recipient, based on an application submitted by the Ghana County Coordination M with the support of the MOH, GHS/NMCP, WHO and PMI. The PMI and AGA programs in IRS have collaborated frequently over the years in areas such as training and community mobilization and continue to share best practices in operations, M&E, and procurement. As members of the Malaria Vector Control Oversight Committee, each organization contributed to developing the country's first *Standard Operating Procedures for IRS (2011)*.

Within USG

PMI functions within the GHI strategy and collaborates with other USG agencies supporting malaria control in Ghana such as Peace Corps, Centers for Disease Control (CDC), Naval Medical Research Unit, Department of Defense, National Institutes of Health, and the State

Department. Peace Corps volunteers are posted to United States Agency for International Development (USAID) projects to support community mobilization and promote malaria control interventions. Peace Corps volunteers have been particularly engaged in the LLIN distribution campaigns and selected PMI operational research. The Department of Defense, National Institutes of Health, and Naval Medical Research Unit support malaria vaccine research, surveillance of incidence and causes of fevers, laboratory system strengthening for infectious disease, and drug resistance monitoring. The CDC under the President's Emergency Plan for AIDS Relief continues to coordinate its technical assistance in strategic information, Field Epidemiologic and Laboratory Training Program (FELTP), and laboratory system strengthening.

The USG supports integrated health programs in Ghana to strengthen health systems while addressing specific goals in maternal and child health (MCH), nutrition, reproductive health, water and sanitation, malaria, and HIV/AIDS. In three regions, covering one third of Ghana's population, USAID Ghana works at the community, district, and regional levels to encourage positive behavior change, improve the quality of service delivery, and improve health management systems, thereby achieving results across the full spectrum of health elements. USAID Ghana aims to expand its integrated health programming into two additional regions by 2014. PMI-supported malaria programming has been integrated into these region-specific efforts to ensure that malaria-specific content is strengthened (e.g. in training and quality assurance) and that health system strengthening will lead to improvement in malaria control indicators (e.g. improved availability of LLINs and ACTs). In addition, PMI will support expanded case management interventions through the Systems for Health Project to ensure the entire country is covered.

PMI support to strengthen commodity supply chains is combined with USG funding under President's Emergency Plan for AIDS Relief and other GHI areas, as a concerted effort to improve supply chains for all pharmaceuticals and health commodities. PMI's contributions and technical assistance to IPTp is integrated with the antenatal care (ANC) program and includes support to strengthen training institutions for midwives throughout the country. Support for case management provided in concert with capacity building for management of other childhood illnesses, such as diarrhea and respiratory infections, brings added value to both PMI and MCH programs.

PMI GOALS, TARGETS, AND INDICATORS

The goal of PMI is to reduce malaria-associated mortality by 70% compared to pre-Initiative levels in the 15 original PMI countries and to reduce malaria-associated mortality by 50% in new countries added to the PMI in FY2010 and later. By the end of 2014, PMI will assist Ghana to achieve the following targets in populations at risk for malaria:
- >90% of households with a pregnant woman and/or children under five will own at least 1 ITN;
- 85% of children under five will have slept under an ITN the previous night;
- 85% of pregnant women will have slept under an ITN the previous night;
- 85% of houses in geographic areas targeted for IRS will have been sprayed;
- 85% of pregnant women and children under five will have slept under an ITN the previous night or in a house that has been sprayed with IRS in the last 6 months;

- 85% of women who have completed a pregnancy in the last 2 years will have received 2 or more doses of IPTp during that pregnancy;
- 85% of government health facilities have ACTs available for treatment of uncomplicated malaria

EXPECTED RESULTS – YEAR SIX

Prevention:
- Procure and distribute approximately 300,000 LLINs through Expanded Program on Immunization (EPI), ANC and school-based distribution systems.
- Protect a population of at least 600,000 residents through IRS in select districts, as determined by the results of the scoping study.
- Support the pre-service training, in-service training and supportive supervision to maintain and improve IPTp rates. Fill in gaps for SP as needed.

Treatment
- Procure and support distribution of approximately 5.5 million RDTs.
- Support the supervision and on the job training for at least 500 laboratory personnel and 205 laboratories annually.
- Procure and support distribution of approximately 7.8 million treatments of pediatric ACTs and severe malaria medicines as required.

PROGRESS ON COVERAGE/IMPACT INDICATORS TO DATE

As in many African countries, PMI and the NMCP rely on nationally representative health surveys to track progress in coverage of malaria control interventions in Ghana. There have been four such surveys since 2003, each implemented by the Ghana Statistical Service and partners, and each conducted during the late rainy season, albeit during different months and in some cases employing slightly different methods. The 2003 DHS was conducted in July-October and the 2006 MICS in August-October. The 2008 DHS, conducted September-November 2008, provides the baseline for key PMI indicators.

The 2011 MICS incorporated a full malaria module and was conducted in September-December 2011. Called the *2011 Ghana MICS4 with Enhanced Malaria Module and Biomarkers*, this latest survey was led by Ghana Statistical Service and UNICEF, with PMI and the NMCP supporting a robust malaria module through technical assistance, funding, and oversight. Although the 2003 and 2008 DHS included anemia testing, a new feature in the 2011 MICS is the inclusion of malaria prevalence data (both microscopic and RDT-based). The survey provides a unique nationwide snapshot of peak season malaria point-prevalence in children age 6-59 months (Figure 1). The Navrongo Health Research Center was contracted to implement the anemia and parasitemia components.

Ghana has achieved steady gains in many of the key malaria intervention indicators, as indicated in Table A. Between 2003 and 2011, ITN ownership and use, uptake of IPTp, and treatment with ACTs have all increased. A universal LLIN campaign was conducted in 2012, and pilots of routine distribution through schools, ANC, and EPIs will occur in 2013. Based on these additional vector control efforts since the 2011 MICS, the next DHS scheduled for 2014 should show an increase in ITN ownership and use.

Table A. Recent Estimates of Malaria Indicators				
Indicator	2003 DHS	2006 MICS	2008 DHS	2011 MICS
Proportion of households with one or more ITN	3%	19%	33%	49%
Proportion of children under five years old who slept under an ITN the previous night	4%	22%	28%	39%
Proportion of pregnant women who slept under an ITN the previous night	3%	NA	20%	33%
Proportion of women who received two or more doses of IPTp during their last pregnancy in the last two years*	0	28%	44%	64%
Proportion of children under five years old with fever in the last two weeks who received treatment with ACTs*	NA	3%	12%	18%**
Under-five Mortality	111	111	80	82

* SP was adopted for IPTp in 2003 ACTs were adopted in 2004.

** The 2011 MICS did not distinguish adequately between responses for "amodiaquine" (23.6%) and "artesunate-amodiaquine," which was counted along with arthemeter-lumefantrin, dihydroartemisinin – piperaquine as "any ACT" (18%). Thus, the true figure may lie somewhere between 18% and an estimated 36%. Supporting this conclusion, government health centers and CHPS compounds were found to prescribe an implausible 55.6% "amodiaquine." Moreover, it has emerged that in popular speech, artesunate-amodiaquine is often called "amodiaquine."

CHALLENGES, OPPORTUNITIES, AND THREATS

Ghana has a technically sound national strategy and strong leadership from the NMCP. With support from PMI, the Global Fund, and other partners, Ghana has established strong malaria control guidelines and trained more than 13,000 healthcare workers throughout the country in case management and malaria in pregnancy (MIP). Ghana has resources, through the Global Fund, to expand IRS to cover up to one fourth of the districts in the country. The gains from these activities can be seen in improved malaria control indicators detailed above in Table A. National surveys indicate that Ghana has made significant progress over the past few years to increase LLIN ownership and use and to increase IPTp uptake. Progress in prompt case management with diagnostics and ACTs has progressed more slowly. While coverage and usage rates are increasing, they still fall well below targets (except for IPTp). Also, a mass ITN campaign took place at the end of 2012 and therefore was not reflected in the 2011 MICS.

The threat of emerging resistance – by the vector to insecticides and by the parasite to artemisinin-based drugs –is a concern for Ghana. Resistance to multiple classes of pesticides is well known in southern Ghana (associated with intensive pesticide use in cocoa production and other farming activities) and elsewhere in West Africa. PMI has taken measures such as changing pesticide class in the IRS program and incorporating enhanced testing for resistance in the 2012 IRS work plan. The NMCP has also identified an insecticide resistance management strategy as a priority. PMI has committed seed money and technical assistance for Malaria Vector Control Oversight Committee to establish a nationwide network for insecticide resistance surveillance. The network secretariat would be housed at the Noguchi Institute.

PMI continues to support vigilance to guard against drug resistance by promoting the rational use of ACTs; sponsoring periodic *in vivo* drug efficacy studies; and supporting efforts to detect sub-standard and counterfeit drugs.

Knowledge about malaria transmission and prevention among the general population continues to pose a significant challenge to malaria control in Ghana. According to the 2011 MICS, 86% of Ghanaians know that malaria is transmitted though mosquito bites. However, well over 50% of Ghanaians (55% of women and 58% of men surveyed) think malaria is also caused by dirty surroundings. There is a well-ingrained mythology, perpetuated in schools and in the media, that malaria control has everything to do with reducing filth and littering. Other frequently mentioned causes of malaria included standing or working in the sun (sited by 44% of men in the Volta Region) and eating contaminated food (sited by 24% of women in the Central Region). A high percentage of Ghanaians identified keeping the environment clean as protective against malaria (60% of men and 58% of women).

Despite significant economic growth over the past 20 years and a demonstrated capacity to advance democracy through five successive peaceful elections, Ghana faces persistent development challenges which, according to the recently published USAID Country Development Cooperation Strategy 2013-2017, "must be addressed to realize and sustain the benefits of a middle-income country." Challenges cited which are largely outside the influence of PMI and the NMCP, yet would have clear implications for malaria control include: (1) "a strong geographic disparity in income," whereby the poverty rate is about 20% in the south, but 60% in the north; (2) the potentially destabilizing socio-economic and political effects of the recently exploited oil reserves; (3) failure so far to reach its potential in good governance, with weak institutions, corruption, and other constraints to providing Ghanaians with required services; and (4) cross-cutting challenges in the health sector, including mismanagement of health commodities and human resources and limited access to and quality of health services.

PMI SUPPORT STRATEGY

The PMI/Ghana strategy includes all of the major interventions supported by PMI. The emphasis and level of support for each of the interventions takes into consideration the contributions from the GOG, Global Fund, DfID, and other stakeholders to ensure priority interventions are scaled up, gaps are filled, and regional variations in malaria epidemiology and progress to-date are addressed.

Since the Global Fund financing is uncertain after February 2015 and recognizing the limited progress on prompt treatment with ACTs, the FY 2014 MOP priorities include procurement of pediatric formulations of ACTs and RDTs and enhanced technical assistance for case management. The PMI strategy will also take a more targeted approach to implementing interventions based on new information from the MICS parasite prevalence and malaria control intervention data, as well as the anemia and parasitemia study from the IRS district. For example, expensive prevention efforts, such as door-to-door ITN distribution and media campaigns, will be a lower priority for PMI in Greater Accra Region, which has the lowest parasite prevalence (4%) of the ten regions, compared to Northern Region with an estimated 48% parasite prevalence and moderate LLIN use (38% among pregnant women and 42% among children under five years old). Investing in universal confirmatory testing to promote rational use of ACTs will be a higher priority in Greater Accra (11% confirmatory testing) than Upper East Region with an estimated 44% parasite prevalence and 36% confirmatory testing.

The LLIN strategy has shifted from mass campaigns to support for routine LLIN distribution, including both school-based mini-campaigns and distribution at ANC and child-welfare clinics. Malaria stakeholders implemented universal coverage campaigns in all 10 regions by December 2012. Sustaining the gains made through the campaigns is now the priority. PMI will concentrate community mobilization and communications to promote LLIN use in regions where the need is greatest (e.g. large rural population and high parasite prevalence) and the potential for gains is highest (e.g. low existing net use and large population size).

PMI's IRS activity in the Northern Region has highlighted the complex relationships between parasite, environment, vector and host. The spraying has had a positive impact on vector-related transmission factors, but, to date, an unclear impact on morbidity. However, the anticipated completion of numerous M&E activities in late 2013 is expected to yield data that will better explain this situation and inform future IRS strategies.

The Global Fund IRS program is expected to reach full scale in 2014-2015 and will cover 26 districts. The PMI technical support for IRS and related entomological monitoring continues to be important to vector control stakeholders in Ghana and is expected to continue to make valuable contributions to future IRS scale up by maximizing program learning and capacity building. However, after six years of spraying in a set of rural districts in the northern savannah (2008-2013), PMI is exploring options for alternative targeting of the intervention and benefitting other areas of Ghana. Pyrethroid insecticide resistance has emerged in the target area, leading to a seven-fold increase in the cost of pesticide and necessitating a scale back in areas covered in 2013. The epidemiologic data available to date suggest that the impact of IRS on morbidity has been modest at best. IRS targeting in calendar year 2014 and 2015 will be based on the recommendations of the ongoing national scoping exercise, the analysis of a recently completed 3-year study of community parasite rates in an IRS district, and data generated by the epidemiologic and entomologic monitoring conducted PMI and AGA/Global Fund IRS programs. This enhanced M&E will contribute to increased understanding of the reasons underlying the persistently high parasite prevalence in Northern Region and options for addressing it.

PMI has been the NMCP's lead partner supporting malaria prevention during pregnancy and will continue to provide technical assistance for IPTp and fill gaps for SP if required. The IPTp activities will solidify gains through supportive supervision and will focus on integrated ANC support, ANC outreach, and community mobilization and behavior change activities in regions where the IPTp rate is lagging, such as the Volta Region.

In FY 2013 and FY 2014, PMI is significantly increasing the proportion of the budget supporting malaria case management, and RDT and ACT procurements. Drawing on concerns about adequate supplies of quality pediatric formulations of ACTs, past stock-outs of RDTs, and uncertainty about the future Global Fund grant, PMI will considerably increase procurement of ACTs and RDTS. PMI will also contribute to the integrated USAID activity to reform the GOG pharmaceutical procurement and supply system. The PMI strategy will continue to solidify the gains from training health workers in the malaria case management guidelines through supportive supervision and quality improvement while shifting the emphasis for new activities to rural and peripheral health services. The PMI strategy will support expansion of the CHPS program and enhancing the quality of the malaria case management services. The PMI strategy will also include a private sector activity to enhance pharmacy and LCS compliance.

III. TECHNICAL SECTIONS

INSECTICIDE-TREATED NETS (ITN)

NMCP/PMI Objectives

The NMCP's objective for ITNs is universal coverage for the entire population, defined as one LLIN for every two people (adjusted to 1.8 people to account for households with odd number of occupants). The distribution strategy includes door-to-door distribution campaigns and routine distribution. The campaigns are conducted region by region on a rolling basis. The routine distribution system, when fully implemented, will include ANC, EPIs, schools, non-governmental organizations (NGOs) and the private sector. At the end of 2012, rolling campaigns were held in Ghana with door -to-door distribution with a hang-up component. The post campaign 'keep-up' strategy is routine distribution involving the use of three principal channels: ANC, EPI, and school-based distributions. The NMCP also supports communication and community mobilization activities to promote consistent ITN use, with a target of 85% of pregnant women and children under five years of age sleeping under an ITN every night.

Progress During the Last 12 Months

Ghana completed its nationwide universal LLIN coverage campaign at the end of 2012. The door-to-door distribution campaigns distributed more than 12.4 million LLINs to households in all ten regions.

The NMCP's routine distribution strategy relies on EPI, ANC and school-based distribution channels. Using NetCalc as the tool for projecting the country's LLIN needs, it is estimated that the school based distribution channel will contribute 45% towards maintaining universal coverage, while EPI and ANC will contribute 29% and 26% respectively—resulting in projected coverage rates of 90% in 2013 and 85% in 2014.

With PMI support, NMCP conducted a pilot of the routine distribution approach to test the suitability of schools, ANC, and EPI clinics as distribution channels. The pilot was conducted in the Eastern and Volta Regions between October 2012 and February 2013. The distribution targeted children in classes 2 and 6 in schools, first registrants at ANCs, and children under 18 months coming in for the second measles booster dose. A total of 181,600 nets were distributed to children in 2,683 public and private schools. Circuit supervisors from 183 circuits in all 21 districts in the Eastern region supervised 5,300 teachers who distributed the nets and provided education on the use and care of the nets to the school children. More than 99% of targeted school children in classes 2 and 6 received nets during the pilot school-based distribution. Coverage rates for EPI and ANC were 98% and 50% (low rate of this category was attributed to under reporting). Based on the coverage rates achieved and the exceptionally good level of cooperation from school authorities, the NMCP decided to scale up the distribution of LLIN nationwide using these three channels.

Healthcare workers at ANC and EPI distribution centers were trained in all regions in the country. Distribution of LLINs through ANC and EPI visits is ongoing in five of the ten regions that were first covered by the mass campaign. The remaining regions will be covered within the year through a phased approach. Trainings for the scale up of the school-based distribution have begun nationwide, and distribution of LLINs will be rolled out simultaneously in all regions between June and August 2013.

From May 2012 to May 2013, PMI procured 2.9 million LLINs for Ghana in support of both universal coverage campaigns and routine distribution. PMI has supported community mobilization and mass media communications (radio and television) to reinforce the campaigns and promote LLIN use and care, in order to reach 85% of the population with behavior change communication (BCC) messages.

Challenges, Opportunities, and Threats

The completion of the universal coverage of ITNs campaign in 2012 dramatically increased LLIN ownership and provided a significant opportunity upon which to build a sustainable routine LLIN distribution system.

Specific challenges to sustaining universal coverage are logistics management issues related to the multiple channels for continuous distribution i.e. school-based, ANC and EPI. Provider training and education on the use and care of nets are also ongoing challenges. Lastly, a revision of ANC forms to include nets distributed will be necessary to prevent continued under reporting through this channel. PMI will need to work with the NMCP and Public Health Division of the MOH to determine appropriate timing for the revision and reprinting of these forms while seeking alternative means of collecting required data.

Despite these challenges, the GHS is poised to sustain the campaign gains through this revised and enhanced routine LLIN distribution system. LLIN promotion activities will build on the high volume of LLINs in communities. The school-based distribution has the potential to contribute significantly toward sustaining universal coverage while inculcating a culture of net use in a new generation. If routine distributions prove inadequate to sustain universal coverage, Ghana will likely need to re-introduce targeted campaigns, reviving the region to region approach.

LLIN Gap Analysis

The routine distribution system is being scaled up to cover all ten regions in 2013. An estimated 700,000 LLINs left over from the campaigns were used to start the scale up of the continuous distribution in health facilities and schools. In FY 2013, PMI plans to procure 2.6 million LLINs for continuous distribution. Another 820,000 nets have been procured by the Global Fund. In 2014, the estimated total need through the three channels is 3,510,210. In 2015, the total need is estimated to be approximately 3,595,565.

The NMCP guideline for routine LLIN distribution recommends procuring LLINs in bulk to benefit from economies of scale, with shipments twice a year covering a six-month supply. The LLIN shipments will be divided and transported to regional medical stores upon receipt at the Central Medical Stores. According to the guidelines, ANC and EPI clinics will initially receive a two-month supply of LLINs, and thereafter will request monthly shipments based on consumption during the previous month, maintaining a one-month buffer.

The Global Fund Phase II grant is a two-year grant ending in February 2015. Due to incomplete negotiation between the NMCP and Global Fund, it is not certain how many nets will be procured under this phase of the Global Fund grant and how many nets will be available to the NMCP after the expiration of the grant. Based on planned PMI FY 2013 funding and anticipated Global Fund financing through February 2015, the LLIN gap is minimal and is estimated to be as follows:

Table B. Projected Inventory and gap analysis of LLINs

YEAR	2013	2014	2015
Balance at Start of Year	700,000	693,073	3,203,857
NetCalc Country Need	(3,426,927)	(3,510,210)	(3,595,565)
PMI	2,600,000	800,000	300,000
Global Fund	820,000	5,220,994	0
Balance at End of Year	693,073	3,203,857	(91,708)

Plans and Justification

PMI will procure LLINs for distribution through routine systems and provide technical and financial support to the NMCP and Ghana Education Service (GES) to train staff and implement the routine LLIN distribution system. In FY 2013, PMI will provide direct financing to GHS (NMCP) and Ghana Education Service (GES) to implement the routine system in at least one region through a government-to-government (G2G) mechanism. In FY 2014, PMI intends to provide additional direct financing through GHS for implementation of the routine system through the other regions pending successful implementation and management of funds in FY 2013. PMI will continue to provide some technical assistance to support the routine distribution system of LLINs in FY 2013 and FY 2014. Additionally with FY 2014 funding, two LLIN specialists will be seconded to the NMCP for an initial period of two years, to augment their staffing and also provide the necessary technical support in quantification, training and monitoring of distribution activities.

The NMCP provided significant leadership in the field during the mass campaigns and scale up of the routine system and coordinated the efforts of all the partners involved in the campaigns including USAID, DfID, UNICEF and NGOs. The program is adequately equipped with skilled staff, has logistics and relationships with Regional level staff in GHS and GES, and has demonstrated the capacity to take on more responsibility. The School Health Education Program (SHEP) demonstrated exceptional commitment during the pilot and continues to be a valued partner for the school based distribution.

The NetCALC tool projects that the quantifications for the planned continuous LLIN distribution system will be sufficient to maintain universal coverage of LLINs (one LLIN for every two people in the country) at or above 90% through 2016. In addition, retail distribution by the private sector is widespread in urban areas. The NMCP is opposed to co-payment in public facilities and has no plans as yet for resumption of subsidized, community-based distribution in the private sector.

PMI will continue to support community mobilization and mass media campaigns to create awareness about routine LLIN distribution, LLIN care, and to promote ITN use. Further detail on communications strategy, background and rationale for promotion of LLIN use and maintenance is covered in the BCC section of the MOP (see below).

Proposed activities with FY 2014 funding ($3,270,000)

- Procure and transport LLINs: ($1,500,000)

  Procure a minimum of 300,000 LLINs at an average cost of $5 per LLIN (including the cost of transporting LLINs to distribution points) for distribution to maintain universal coverage. This will cover an estimated 8% of national need, complementing nets contributed by Global Fund and potentially others. These nets are intended to support routine distribution.

- Technical assistance for LLIN distribution and supply chain: ($1,270,000)

  Contingent on successful implementation through G2G mechanisms with GHS in FY 2013, PMI will expand direct financing and technical assistance to GHS and the GES to implement the routine LLIN distribution through ANC, EPI, and schools nationwide. This will include training healthcare to distribute and document distribution of nets, as well as working with GES and schools throughout the country to distribute and promote nets through the school-based distribution channel. Technical assistance through an implementing partner will continue to support the NMCP and provide additional support, as needed, to ensure the routine distribution system remains well functions well.

- Behavior change communications: ($500,000) (see BCC section)

  Building on existing LLIN BCC materials, PMI will support GHS and GES to implement communications activities to promote LLIN ownership and use, employing an evidence-based approach. PMI will support community mobilization, radio and television spots, and communications materials. Particular focus will be placed on net care and misperceptions about use. Technical assistance will be provided to the NMCP, the National Malaria Communications Committee, and SHEP. Support will be channeled through a USAID project in addition to G2G mechanisms.

INDOOR RESIDUAL SPRAYING (IRS)

NMCP/PMI Objectives

Ghana's National Strategic Plan for Malaria Control (2008-2015) calls for rapid scale up of IRS to one-third of the country's 212 districts. This ambitious national IRS objective is based on 2006 WHO recommendations and on the positive experience of the AGA mining company's program in Obuasi municipality (forest zone) since 2005. PMI began supporting IRS in Ghana in 2007, with a focus on local capacity building, strict environmental compliance, and entomological monitoring. In consultations with GHS, a cluster of districts in the Northern Region was selected for spraying due to their high malaria burden, its underserved and vulnerable populations, and the North's relatively short transmission season (which was presumed to allow for one spray campaign per year if a long-acting pesticide formulation is used).

Within the first two years, the PMI IRS program demonstrated that IRS can be scaled up quickly and safely in the more remote rural areas of the country. In 2008, working in close collaboration with GHS and local communities, the program protected 601,000 people in 5 districts. By 2011, the program had expanded to cover a population of 926,000 in 9 districts. Each year, the program exceeded the 90% national targets for coverage of local structures found.

To contribute toward the NMCP and PMI objective of national IRS capacity-building, PMI facilitated the establishment of a national Malaria Vector Control Committee, helped the NMCP to coordinate and guide IRS implementation in the country. The committee includes partners such as AGA, the Noguchi Institute, the Environmental Protection Agency and other IRS partners and has proven to be a dynamic, well attended forum which has been meeting quarterly since 2009. The committee aids the NMCP in meeting national objectives for quality control, environmental compliance, and insecticide resistance management has established and disseminated national IRS standard operating procedure, and facilitated information exchange and coordination of effort.

Ghana is the beneficiary of a five-year, approximately $130 million Global Fund grant to further scale up IRS with AGA as the Principal Recipient. Since 2005, AGA has maintained an integrated malaria control program in Obuasi, which includes IRS, larviciding, and improved housing, near its mines in Obuasi. AGA's program and its outcomes have been held up as a model for malaria control. The company has formed a not-for-profit subsidiary, AGA Malaria Control Ltd., to implement IRS under the Global Fund grant. Beginning with 7 districts in 2012, the AGA program was conducting biannual spraying in 17 districts by mid-2013. The program appears to be on track to meet its target of scaling up to 22 districts by the end of the 2013, of which 2/3 are in Upper West and Upper East (savannah zone) and the rest are located in Ashanti, Western, and other southern regions (forest and coastal zones).

As AGA/Global Fund has become the largest implementer of IRS in the country, PMI's overall objective has shifted from scale up to maintenance of high quality operations, with a focus on efficacy monitoring, optimization of design, and targeting for increased impact. With Malaria Vector Control Oversight Committee helping to institutionalize a culture of evidence-based decision making in IRS, both the AGA/Global Fund and PMI programs have increased their investments in entomologic and epidemiologic monitoring over time.

Progress During the Last 12 Months

In 2012, the PMI-funded spray operations reached 941,240 people, including 21,774 pregnant women and 188,696 children under five, in 9 districts. Teams operating from 31 operational sites in 9 contiguous districts of Northern Region sprayed 383,142 structures, exceeding the target of 90% coverage. The program provided seasonal employment to almost 1,000 people from local communities in 2012. A cumulative total of over 2,500 IRS implementers have been trained, and management capacity continued to be built at district, regional, and national levels.

The program is continuing to mature as it enters its sixth spray round, with increasing emphasis on evaluation, monitoring, and quality control. The database for tracking IRS operations has been upgraded, additional entomologic monitoring sites have been added, and a number of research activities are being undertaken. Enhanced entomologic monitoring, undertaken in collaboration with the Noguchi Institute, has demonstrated a shift to a younger population of female *Anopheles* (reflective of increased mosquito mortality due to the pesticides). Data from community monitoring sites have documented a ten-fold reduction in entomological inoculation rates, which measures the number of mosquito bites per person per night.

Across the five spray rounds of 2008-2012, entomologic monitoring detected the gradual emergence of pyrethroid resistance (Figure 3). In 2012, a team comprised of members from PMI, Noguchi Institute, GHS, Malaria Vector Control Oversight Committee and NMCP analyzed entomological data. This prompted the team's decision to transition to a long-acting organophosphate. Although six to seven times more expensive than the pyrethroids and carbamate-class insecticides, organophosphates were selected as the most effective and appropriate class given their residual effect and the susceptibility of the local vectors. In 2012, three of the nine districts were sprayed with a long-acting organophosphate, Actellic CS 300 (pirimiphos methyl). Monthly wall bio-assays demonstrated pesticide efficacy of at least 6-8 months, which was comparable to the pyrethroids previously used.

Also in 2012, a PMI-supported operations research study continued in Bunkpurugu-Yunyoo district, the designated study district. In collaboration with Noguchi Institute, PMI has compared the effectiveness of one vs. two annual rounds of spraying in the northern savannah zone. Baseline surveys of malaria and anemia prevalence in children were conducted in the study district during the 2010 peak and trough transmission seasons. During both the 2011 and 2012 seasons, half the district was sprayed once and half the district twice, with malaria and anemia surveys conducted during the annual peak and trough transmission seasons. Ongoing data analysis suggests that both halves of the district experienced a modest (approx. 25%) decrease in parasite prevalence rates from baseline to IRS in year 2. The final data collection for this study was completed in April 2013. Findings regarding the benefit of one vs. two spray rounds are pending, awaiting the incorporation of data from the last survey and full analysis. A report is expected by late 2013.

In the past year, additional epidemiologic impact data was also collected from the busiest hospital in the IRS zone, namely Nalerigu BMC Hospital in East Mamprusi District (>85% pediatric malaria cases from IRS districts; 20,068 admissions; 99,555 slides). A published review of six years of Nalerigu data showed no decrease in annual malaria admissions, the proportion of malaria admissions, positive slides, or slide positivity rate in the three years that IRS has been conducted. Data from a fourth year, which followed the switch to an organophosphate, show a modest decrease in some of these parameters and is being analyzed further.

Meanwhile, the AGA/Global Fund IRS program began reporting data from its newly established sentinel sites with a protocol that specifies testing of all "suspected" malaria cases with RDTs one week per month in three clinics per IRS district. AGA/Global Fund also conducted pre-IRS, school-based prevalence studies in two districts. The main objective of this study is to provide baseline measures of parasitemia prevalence in two districts prior to AGA/Global Fund IRS spraying and compare the data to post-IRS activities, which are scheduled during the 2013 rainy season. However, pre-IRS vs. post-IRS, year-on-year comparison data from AGA/ Global Fund will not be available until late 2013 or early 2014.

Based on resistance data and on the favorable 2012 experience, the decision was made to use the long-acting organophosphate, Actellic CS 300 (pirimiphos methyl) in all PMI-supported IRS target districts in 2013. Due to the high cost, this led to a reduction in covered districts from nine to four and a reduction in target coverage to 471,000 structures and 193,000 people.

To ensure a responsible withdrawal of IRS from the five districts where spraying was suspended in 2013, the following steps were taken: (1) stakeholder consultations with local stakeholders, including public health officials, traditional leaders; (2) ensuring universal coverage of ITNs via a media campaign in August 2012 (3) enhanced community-level BCC to promote ITN use and prompt case management; (4) ensuring adequate local ACT stocks to prevent stock-outs; and (5) monthly entomologic monitoring of vector populations.

Figure 3. Summary of insecticide susceptibility test results

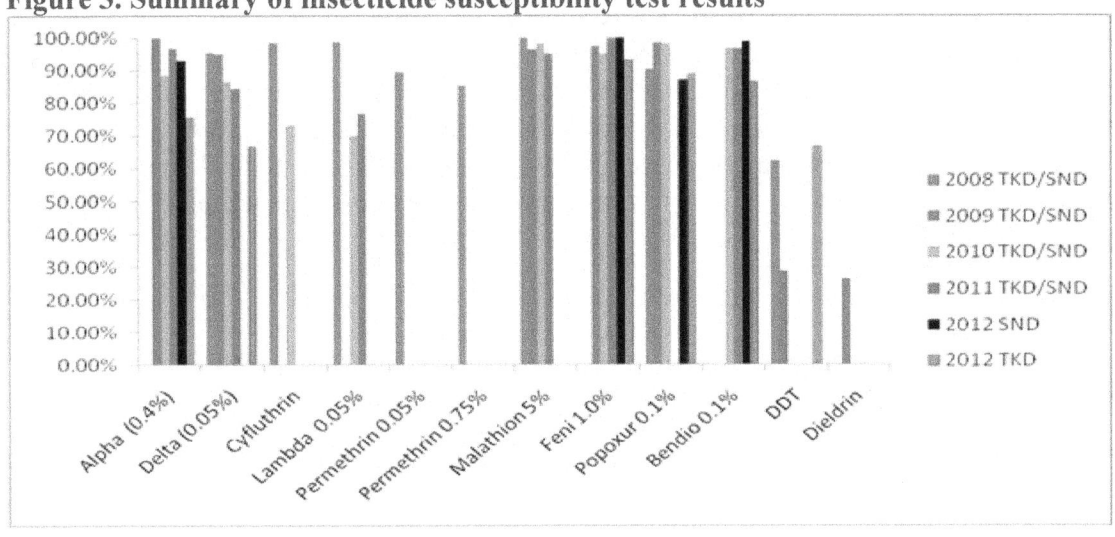

Mean proportion knockdown and mortalities of Anopheles gambiae s.l. in Tolon/Kumbungu and Savelugu Nanton districts exposed to diagnostic doses of different insecticides

Challenges, Opportunities, and Threats

In 2012 and again in 2013, the PMI spray season was delayed due to problems with the supply chain and acquisition of organophosphates. In 2012, a delay in the delivery of the insecticide resulted in only three districts being sprayed with organophosphates, as opposed to the planned six districts. Therefore, spraying was conducted in late July – past the optimal period for spraying. In 2013, the pesticides arrived in Ghana, but due to unforeseen issues, remained at the port for over six weeks, causing a three-week delay in spraying. Nevertheless, the program successfully implemented the transition to the new product, maintaining high coverage rates and strong community acceptance.

In addition to the remote terrain and poor road conditions in the Northern Region, limited local demographic and geographic data sources pose challenges to planning and monitoring. The remarkably strong human capacity with locally hired and effective spray teams, managers, district and regional officials, community health volunteers, and traditional leaders compensated for challenges in this region.

Despite evidence of high quality implementation and favorable entomologic findings, the PMI IRS activity in Northern Region has not yet demonstrated epidemiological impact according to preliminary analysis of several types of epidemiologic data, including routine aggregate district data (DHIMS), longitudinal health facility data, and the serial surveys of community prevalence. High rates of outdoor biting pre-IRS, low availability of ACTs, and practices of sleeping both indoors and outdoors during most nights have been noted in the targeted areas.

In light of these concerns, PMI is supporting efforts to provide the other information that can be used to improve and inform programmatic operations, namely: (1) A "Scoping Exercise" is being conducted by the Liverpool School of Tropical Medicine under the direction of Malaria Vector Control Oversight Committee. It seeks to better define the criteria under which IRS is likely to achieve its highest impact and more specifically, which locations in Ghana meet those criteria – including epidemiologic, entomologic, human behavioral, and logistical considerations. Following a desk review in early 2013 and a stakeholders' workshop, the exercise is progressing to fieldwork stage in mid-2013 and is expected to issue its report by September. (2) A rapid assessment of outdoor sleeping habits in two northern savannah districts has been submitted for IRB approval; it will examine the extent of unprotected outdoor nighttime activity by the residents during a period of high malaria transmission. Finally, (3) a longitudinal analysis of existing entomological data from the Northern Region will be performed to complement the sleeping habits study.

Plans and Justification

IRS experiences in Ghana have raised questions about how best to target IRS, and in particular whether the rural northern savannah is the most appropriate site for IRS. However, NMCP and PMI Ghana have agreed that further investigations are needed to better clarify the impact and role of IRS in different epidemiological and entomological areas, as well as in the context of a multi-pronged approach to malaria control. Under the aegis of Ghana's Malaria Vector Control

Oversight Committee, the PMI team is working collaboratively with stakeholders to develop strategies on the best way forward.

PMI will continue to play a critical role in building national capacity for IRS and informing the national strategy. However, in light of the unresolved questions on efficacy and optimal targeting, it is not possible to justify an increase in IRS budgetary investment above the average recent spending level (calendar year 2011-13).

During the MOP FY 2014 planning process, definitive epidemiologic data was unavailable to inform IRS strategy for calendar years 2014 and 2015. However, by November 2013, the following data and reports are expected, among others, and will be used to decide on target areas and program approach in the 2014 season work plan:

i. Routine entomologic monitoring will provide updated data on insecticide susceptibility and trends in entomological inoculation rates and other parameters. A recently commenced longitudinal analysis of 2008-13 entomologic monitoring data will be available.

ii. The PMI operations research study (on one vs. two spray rounds) in Bunkpurugu-Yunyoo District is expected to shed light on local malaria epidemiology and IRS impact.

iii. A follow-up anemia and parasitemia survey planned for October 2013 in Bunkpurugu-Yunyoo is expected to capture the effect of 2013 IRS program changes, including the change to an organophosphate, coupled with an earlier and more compressed spray season. Preliminary results (RDT-based) would be available for comparison with baseline, year one and year two peak seasons.

iv. The AGA/Global Fund program will report to Malaria Vector Control Oversight Committee on its sentinel site and school-based parasitemia data. By November 2013, this data should allow for the first pre-IRS vs. post-IRS comparisons from the AGA program in settings outside Obuasi District.

v. The scoping exercise will have issued its report on refined targeting criteria, with recommended options for potential areas for future IRS targeting.

Proposed activities with FY 2014 funding ($4,604,000)

- Support for IRS program implementation: ($4,570,000)
  In collaboration with GHS and consultation with PMI HQ IRS Team, and with continued focus on capacity building, support IRS implementation and programmatic evaluation in the 4 existing targeted districts. Future targeting of additional districts will be based on the recommendations of the ongoing national scoping exercise, as well as epidemiologic and entomologic monitoring data from PMI and AGA/Global Fund IRS programs.

  Funding will support entomological monitoring, limited epidemiologic monitoring, spray operations, data collection, environmental assessment and compliance monitoring, BCC activities including community mobilization, and logistics. Proposed activities include continued support for procurement of insecticide and equipment; support for supervision

27

by GHS, Environmental Protection Agency, and Noguchi Memorial Institute personnel; and collaboration with the NMCP, the Malaria Vector Control Oversight Committee, the Global Fund/AGA IRS program, and other partners.

- <u>CDC expert TDY visits and provision of supplies to support entomologic monitoring for IRS:</u> ($34,000)
  Provide technical assistance and quality assurance, through two visits by CDC entomologist, for ongoing entomologic monitoring of the PMI-funded IRS program. To include further assessment of entomologic factors that might be limiting IRS impact in the north, as well as technical assistance to establish entomologic monitoring in any new target areas(s). This includes limited funding for test equipment and supplies. In addition, assist Malaria Vector Control Oversight Committee in implementing a new network of sites for insecticide resistance monitoring nationwide.

MALARIA IN PREGNANCY

NMCP/PMI Objectives

The National Guidelines for Malaria in Pregnancy recommend a multi-pronged approach to the prevention and treatment of malaria during pregnancy. Three major strategies guide the approach: IPTp, vector management strategies (namely ensuring the availability and distribution of LLINs as described under the LLIN section), and case management of malaria.

The current GHS policy is to administer three doses of IPTp with SP under directly observed treatment by a health worker. The first dose should be administered at 16 weeks gestation, with each following dose administered at least one month apart and with the last dose administered up to 36 weeks of gestation. Exceptions to the IPTp policy include: pregnant women with glucosephosphate dehydrogenase deficiency or severe liver disease; women who have received treatment with a sulphanamide drug within the past four weeks; and/or HIV-positive women who have been put on co-trimoxazole for opportunistic infections. The GHS guidelines for MIP stress screening of all pregnant women who attend ANC for the first time for reaction to sulpha drugs and exemption from SP if they have a history of reaction to any sulpha drug. The screening process involves a set of six questions related to past sickness and identification of drugs taken. Facilities also stock sulpha drugs to show to pregnant women taking the medication for the first time for identification. Finally, the woman is asked to take the drug before the initiation of the ANC activities so that she could be observed for adverse drug reaction for at least one hour before she leaves the facility.

In October 2012, the WHO revised the IPTp guidelines in line with current evidence to ensure correct SP administration by health workers. The updated recommendations state that SP for all pregnant women should be administered at each scheduled ANC visit, with the first dose administered as early as possible during the second trimester (determined by the onset of quickening or by measurement of fundal height by an ANC health professional). The last dose may be administered up to the time of delivery without safety concerns. Additionally, WHO clarified that folic acid at a daily dose equal or above 5mg should not be given together with SP, as this counteracts its efficacy as an antimalarial. Currently, Ghana administers a dose of 5mg of folic acid daily for pregnant women. PMI is in discussions with NMCP to update its guidelines based on the revised WHO recommendations.

The NMCP's objective is to increase the percentage of women receiving at least two doses of IPTp to 100%. The 2011 MICS data indicate that Ghana has made significant progress towards increasing IPTp rates. The national proportion of women reporting that they received at least two doses of IPTp during their most recent pregnancy in the past two years increased from 44% (2008 DHS) to 64% in 2011 (MICS), although regional disparities exist.

Progress During the Last 12 Months

In order to support the GHS to improve health worker capacity to effectively deliver a package of malaria prevention and care services to pregnant women, PMI has collaborated with NMCP to train more than 2,000 health care providers in IPTp during the last 12 months. Orientation on the revised WHO IPTp recommendations was provided to about 260 providers at one of Ghana's leading teaching hospitals, Korle-Bu. The Public Health Unit at Korle-Bu developed customized guidelines on IPTp in accordance with the updated recommendations for use and dissemination in the Obstetrics Department.

During the past 12 months, PMI projects strengthened the pre-service education for midwives, community and public health nurses by updating technical MIP and IPTp training materials within basic emergency obstetric and newborn care. A total of 38 health professional schools (10 community health nursing schools, 1 public health nursing school, 1 medical assistant training school and 26 midwifery schools) received the pre-service education to improve the knowledge, skills and practices of the GHS MIP guidelines. In support of the DHIMS2 and to strengthen data quality, PMI provided training to 1,532 providers on the revised forms and registers related to the measurement of IPTp indicators. To improve data recording, reporting, and quality, PMI printed revised forms and GHS registers for distribution at health facilities and supported NMCP in conducting Malaria Data Review Meetings.

Challenges, Opportunities, and Threats

Over the past few years, high ANC attendance rates in Ghana have provided great opportunity to achieve the NMCP/PMI IPTp objectives. Based upon the 2011 MICS, 96% of pregnant women reported attending ANC 4 or more times. The MICS also shows that Ghana has made tremendous gains in IPTp coverage over the past few years. In 2011 there was a mass training of health staff at ANC clinics, and this was followed in 2012 with supportive supervision to ensure skills taught were applied correctly. Maintaining strong and regular supportive supervision has the potential to sustain and expand the gains made over the last few years. There is, however, a high attrition rate of trained personnel which requires continuous training.

Currently, in FY 2012, there is a stock-out of SP at many health facilities due to delays in procurement of SP. The GHS policy for procuring and registering SP in Ghana requires the manufacturer to be on a pre-approved list. The manufacturer from which other global donors generally procure is not registered in country. The NMCP plans to secure resources from the

GOG to purchase from local manufacturers to fill the gap, but it is not known whether they will be successful. PMI will make efforts to fill the SP gap in FY 2012 as needed.

Table C. SP Gap Analysis

YEAR	2013	2014	2015
National Public Sector Requirement	3,927,150	7,700,000	6,000,000
Global Fund/Other Fund	3,927,150 *(NB: Delivery in 2013 is in doubt due to anticipated delays)*	5,000,000	0
PMI	0	2,700,000	6,000,000
Gap	0	0	0

Plans and Justification

PMI will continue to sustain and build on increasing IPTp rates for the upcoming year. PMI will support the GHS to continue to strengthen ANC services, update the national policy to be in line with the revised WHO guidance, maintain support for pre-service training, revise training manuals, and promote early and regular ANC attendance.

PMI will use different mechanisms to support MIP activities with FY 2014 funding. PMI will work intensively on all aspects of MIP in five regions, and others regions as needed. The table below lists IPTp coverage rates by region (2011 MICS), from lowest to highest. Regions targeted by PMI for intensive support in IPTp and MIP are highlighted in yellow.

Table D. Percentage of women age 15-49 who received two or more doses of SP/Fansidar during pregnancy within the last two years by region – Ghana MICS, 2011

Region	SP/Fansidar two or more times (%)
Volta	39.3
Western	59.8
Greater Accra	61.6
Brong Ahafo	61.9
Central	65.0
Upper West	65.3
Northern	67.0
Upper East	69.4
Eastern	71.4
Ashanti	75.0

PMI's focus regions for intensive support on IPTp and MIP include the three regions with the lowest current coverage for IPTp. This support is integrated with work to improve focused antenatal care (FANC) overall. Supportive supervision for MIP, as a component of case management, in the other five regions will be supported by PMI through direct financing of Ghana Health Services (see case management section). PMI's main provider of technical assistance will also provide training and policy support on IPTp to the regional health management teams for those districts. DfID focuses on Brong Ahafo Region for technical assistance on reproductive health care, including FANC, and is currently identifying target areas for their malaria work; PMI is recommending Brong Ahafo and Ashanti regions.

The PMI team anticipates that Global Fund or DfID financing will be used to support intensified MIP activities in the other regions but will be able to provide technical assistance and support if required. PMI will scale up case management of malaria in pregnant women and will continue to support pre-service training for IPTp and MIP.

The PMI team anticipates that most of the needs for SP will be covered through the Global Fund Phase 2 grant proposal or through GOG resources; however, PMI is willing to step in to procure SP on an emergency gap basis if the need should arise. The budget for a potential SP gap is included in the Treatment section.

Proposed activities with FY 2014 funding ($1,240,000)

- Strengthen ANC services and in-service training: ($540,000)
  Support the GHS to improve health worker and health system capacity to effectively deliver a package of malaria prevention and care services to pregnant women. PMI support will focus on supportive supervision, on-site training as needed, quality improvement to increase healthcare worker administration of at least three IPTp doses, and support for implementing updated MIP guidance. Intensive support will be targeted to five focus regions, with additional support as needed in the other regions.

- Pre-service training for MIP: ($300,000)
  Provide technical pre-service training for nurses, midwives and medical assistants in the prevention of MIP. Expand activities to general nursing schools as applicable and provide technical assistance towards the development of training manuals. Extend training in current 28 schools to include Tutors for general nursing and increase number of midwifery and general nursing schools supported to 58 schools.

- BCC to promote IPTp: ($400,000)
  Support the distribution and use of communication materials to improve health workers' administration of IPTp. Support community mobilization and communication materials (print and mass media) to promote IPTp with a particular focus on geographic areas and/or cultural groups with low IPTp uptake rates. MIP messages will be incorporated with national health promotion and MCH BCC activities.

CASE MANAGEMENT

Malaria Diagnosis

NMCP/PMI Objectives

More than 50% of all clinic visits in Ghana are due to febrile illnesses. The NMCP policy requires parasitological confirmation of all malaria cases, with priority given to patients under five years old. Reliable malaria testing – whether through microscopy or RDTs – is essential to providing appropriate care to these patients, as well as to providing reliable surveillance. In late 2009, the NMCP began promoting a policy of universal malaria diagnosis (microscopy or RDTs) in all age groups consistent with the new WHO guidelines. Since then, the focus has been on improving the quality of microscopy at the higher-level facilities and scaling up the use of RDTs in peripheral settings, including the CHPS zones. Progress on scaling up diagnostics has been slow and faced challenges, such as RDT stockouts and reluctance of providers to adhere to test results.

Progress During the Last 12 Months

PMI has been working closely with NMCP, the National Public Health Reference Lab, and the GHS Clinical Laboratories Unit (CLU) to improve the quality and scale up of malaria diagnosis in Ghana. PMI has been supporting the Outreach Training and Supportive Supervision (OTSS) program, which consists of periodic rounds of structured supervisory visits to clinical laboratories by regional technical specialists in the GHS. A formalized checklist is used to assess infrastructure, personnel, and efficiency.

The OTSS program has been rolled out systematically across Ghana. All 408 health facilities with a laboratory (as counted in a 2008 assessment) have been enrolled into the OTSS program (these include 302 (74%) public facilities, 45 (11%) private and 61 (15%) public/private facilities). As of January 2013, 9 rounds were completed, reaching a target total of 408 (100% of all labs enrolled) health facilities. In the last twelve months 74% of all lab technicians were trained. Since the program began in 2009, the percentage of laboratory agreement with supervisor microscopy readings (gold standard) has been maintained at over 90%. Refresher training for district supervisors has been ongoing and is supported through the dissemination of a WHO CD-ROM on malaria microscopy for self-practice. PMI also supported the creation of a national archive of malaria slides to support proficiency testing. The slide archive was completed and piloted in the last round of OTSS in Greater Accra and Eastern Regions at the end of 2012.

PMI has also supported the scale up of RDTs through the procurement of RDTs and training of health workers on diagnosis and case management. Over the last 12 months, 2,283 health and community health workers have been trained. In response to reports of RDT stockouts, PMI procured 2.7 million RDTs which arrived in the second and third quarter of 2012. Global Fund financing is covering RDT needs for most of 2013.

Challenges, Opportunities, and Threats

Ensuring sufficient financial resources and averting stockouts of RDTs have been recurring challenges since 2010. Health facility surveys and OTSS data continue to reveal ongoing facility-level RDT stockouts. Diagnostic testing continues to have a suboptimal impact due to persistent RDT stockouts, patient flow bottlenecks in facilities, and lack of provider adherence to test results. There is general sense that physicians remain reluctant to prescribe treatment in accordance with diagnostic results, and additional work needs to be done to reach this cadre of health professionals.

Many patients still seek care in the private sector through LCS who have not been trained nor have access to RDTs. There are Global Fund-financed pilots on deploying RDTs through LCS's that are currently underway that are expected to inform policy decisions on scaling up diagnostics through the private sector.

A major challenge for continued OTSS program scale up is the rapidly increasing number of clinical laboratories, especially in Ghana's thriving private sector that now exceeds 600. Based on recent experience, limitations in qualified supervisors are likely to pose the greatest constraints to scale up. This is being addressed through continued investments in training and certification.

The GHS CLU is responsible for overseeing the management of the diagnostics scale up in conjunction with NMCP. PMI entered into a G2G agreement with the CLU to implement OTSS and integrate the activities within its programs. The FY 2012 planned funding and program activities have been delayed for a variety of factors. PMI will monitor the progress on this activity and mechanism and adjust the mechanism and FY 2013 funding as needed to ensure that activities remain on track.

Plans and Justification

PMI will continue to support the OTSS program and seek mechanisms to further integrate management of this program into the GHS CLU, through direct funding agreements with CLU and technical assistance from implementing partners. Refresher training on microscopy and regular supervisory visits will continue. PMI plans to continue holding four rounds of OTSS per year, each round would cover 205 laboratories across 10 regions and provide on-the-job training to at least 500 laboratory personnel.

PMI will also continue to support the scale up of RDTs with a specific focus on peripheral health facilities and CHPS zones. This will include pre-service and in-service training, and a focus on improving provider compliance and patient demand for diagnostics. Depending on the results of the pilot and policy changes, PMI will also support the roll out of RDTs in the private sector through LCS and pharmacies.

Ghana has just completed negotiating the Global Fund Phase 2 Grant award. Based on the Phase 2 negotiations and preliminary quantification, the RDT gap is estimated to be as follows.

Table D. RDT GAP Analysis - May 2013

	2013	2014	2015
National **Public Sector** Requirement	9,078,128	10,209,003	11,813,133
Global Fund/Other Fund	7,595,700 *(Includes 1,600,000 which may be delivered in 2014)*	7,000,000	0
PMI	3,000,000	1,920,000	5,250,000
Surplus/(Gap)	1,517,572	228,569	(6,334,564)

Proposed activities with FY 2014 funding ($5,062,000)

- Procure RDTs: ($3,300,000)
  Support procurement of around 5 million RDTs and fill 48% of the estimated public sector gap.   Procure limited number of microscopes and microscopy kits to fill gaps in a fast-growing health system.

- Strengthen quality of microscopy and RDT use at laboratory level: ($500,000)
  Continue to support quality improvements to malaria microscopy and RDT use at the laboratory level, building upon and continuing the scale up of the successful OTSS program. Focus on improving the efficiency of testing processes and on using the test results to inform clinical decisions and surveillance. The quality assurance program contains supervisory field visits and on the job training, including proficiency testing using the recently developed slide archive. Provide technical assistance and financing for supportive supervision and on-the-job training of laboratory personnel, complemented by refresher training for lab supervisors. Emphasize transfer of increased management responsibility to the CLU. Pending successful implementation of this approach with FY 2013 funding, FY 2014 funding will be allocated between a direct G2G agreement with the CLU and a USAID technical assistance partner.

- Scale up RDT use in clinical settings: ($1,250,000)
  Accelerate collaborative efforts with the NMCP and GHS at all levels to achieve high rates of parasitological testing, with a focus on scaling up RDT use in clinical settings. Support identification and removal of operational, financial, policy, and other bottlenecks to the use of RDTs. Support capacity building to ensure consistent availability and use of RDTs at public health facilities, particularly CHPS. Building on recent GHS pilot projects and operations research, PMI will support the roll-out of RDTs to community-based agents, LCS and pharmacies as the GHS/ NMCP approves these entities to use RDTs.   PMI will support linkages with National Health Insurance Agency (NHIA) to improve testing rates. PMI will provide technical assistance to Regional Health Directorates to undertake measures such as in-service training, supervision, and reporting

of stockouts. Periodic end user verification surveys will also determine availability and adequacy of supplies at facilities and advise Regional Health Directorates appropriately.

- Provide technical assistance in diagnostics: ($12,000)
  CDC will provide technical assistance to support implementation of microscopy, quality assurance for diagnostics, and RDT implementation.

Treatment

NMCP/PMI Objectives

The NMCP strategy calls for widespread, prompt access to ACTs. Ghana first adopted artesunate-amodiaquine as a first-line therapy for uncomplicated malaria in 2004. Artemether-lumefantrine and dihydroartemisinin-piperaquine are officially endorsed as alternative treatments, and malaria treatment guidelines reflecting this policy were revised in 2008/2009. PMI continues to urge adoption by the MOH of a single first-line ACT, to permit greater efficiency in training, procurement and monitoring, and the NMCP is moving in this direction. ACTs have been classified as over-the-counter medicines since 2009. The current treatment guidelines call for oral quinine for treatment in the first trimester of pregnancy with either oral quinine or ACTs in the second or third trimester. Intravenous artesunate is being considered to replace quinine as the first-line treatment for severe malaria. Rectal artesunate is endorsed for pre-referral use but is only available and used sporadically.

The NMCP has led efforts to improve access to ACTs through training, supervision, and ensuring the NHIA insurance policies for reimbursing ACT treatments are consistent with the national guidelines. Ghana was also designated as an AMFm pilot country, which has enabled subsidized ACTs to become widely available through the private sector LCS. ACTs for the private sector in 2013 are being supported through the AMFm transition funding. The Global Fund Phase 2 grant proposal has allocated funding for ACTs through both the public and private sector.

The NMCP has also been supporting scale up of case management at peripheral levels through the CHPS facilities and a UNICEF-supported pilot of community case management of malaria through community health workers. Although progress was made in developing guidelines and training materials for the integrated community-based case management of fever (iCCM) program, training, supervision and integration with management of acute respiratory illness and diarrhea has not yet occurred on a broad scale. There have been challenges to integrate the community-based management of malaria into the established health delivery system.

Progress During the Last 12 Months

The AMFm pilot came to an end with a transition phase in 2013. Additional funding to support private sector ACTs is being considered in the Global Fund, Phase 2 application. PMI has supplied 2,385,629 pediatric ACT treatments from June 2012 through June 2013 to address shortfall and ensure supply.

PMI's technical assistance to the NMCP in the last year focused primarily on supervision of health care workers (HCWs). Most first-line health workers have received training or orientation on the malaria case management guidelines. In the last 12 months, the number of district level supervisors trained in supportive supervision increased from 361 to 625. These supervisors provided supportive supervision to 21, 586 health workers in more than 2,000 health facilities in 7 regions. A total of 1,557 community-based agents were trained to support the home management of malaria. Additionally, 726 health workers, mostly from health centers and CHPS compounds, were trained on malaria case management. PMI continued to provide support to pre-service training in 32 public health schools (community health nursing, public health nursing, and midwifery schools).

Challenges, Opportunities, and Threats

Progress in malaria case management in Ghana has been slow. Ongoing challenges in improving case management include late presentation of patients, limited geographic access to skilled care, inconsistent supplies of ACTs, public sector procurements (MOH, district, and facility level) of ACTs that have not been WHO pre-qualified, health workers that have not yet been trained on the standard treatment protocols (largely in lower-level facilities, CHPS and hard-to-reach facilities), and pockets of health workers that remain untrained in approved treatment regimens. The 2011 MICS found that 50% of reported fever cases in children did not seek medical care. At the community level, the roll out of the NMCP's iCCM program has been slow. This program has experienced technical and management challenges, has not received support to treat respiratory infections and diarrhea, and has not been well integrated into the GHS system.

Outside the public health care system, ACTs were available, particularly at LCS and pharmacies, due to the AMFm pilot. LCS and pharmacies are a primary source of care for adults. However, based on the Ghana MICS 2011, only 5.5% of parents with febrile children sought care through LCS or pharmacies. Many, if not most of these facilities, also sell non-approved malaria treatments. Funding to support subsidized ACTs through the private sector is provided through the AMFm transition funding and has been requested in the Phase 2 application. There are also pilots currently underway in Ghana that will inform the design options for introducing RDTs into LCS and pharmacies.

Plans and Justifications

PMI will continue to support training, supervision, and quality improvement in overall case management primarily focusing efforts on the CHPS and rural facilities. The CHPS strategy seeks to provide health services through partnerships between the health program, community leaders, and social groups, by posting trained community health nurses in rural areas. These nurses are responsible for providing public health education and outreach, basic case management services, and referrals. "CHPS zones," as the base of operation for a community health nurse is referred to, often consist of a two-room facility with equipment for basic curative and preventive care. Each zone may be staffed with one to two nurses, who often supervise several volunteer assistants. In some areas, CHPS nurses operate out of health clinics and regularly visit the areas for which they are responsible; however, the model officially requires the nurse to be stationed in his or her target community. The CHPS zone is the first, and often the only, health service point accessed by many rural populations who reside far from a higher-level health facility or may not be motivated to seek care. Ghana's CHPS program is an essential tool to decrease disparities in access to care and to ensure effective referral systems.

Given the challenges in scaling up the iCCM program and GHS commitment to expanding reach at the community level through the CHPS platform, PMI decided to focus funding on improving the quality of malaria case management at the CHPS level. In 2012, GHS made progress in its goal of 100% coverage of rural populations with CHPS services, by expanding to 1,034 CHPS zones throughout the country, covering an estimated 40% of the rural population. USAID, with PMI funding and other health funds, supports the expansion and improvement of CHPS services to deliver an expanded package of proven interventions to reduce maternal and child mortality and morbidity, including malaria case management, child health services, and maternal health services (including IPTp). USAID will scale up CHPS coverage to improve access to health care by providing equipment, training and supervisory support to community health officers in these zones, as well as orientation of community leaders to support the establishment and functioning of CHPS in their communities. Specific training on malaria case management will be provided to CHPS nurses. Health facility and district staff tasked with supervising CHPS nurses will be supported to provide appropriate case management supervision and supplies to the CHPS zones for which they are responsible.

With expansion of the CHPS model prioritized by the GHS and supported by PMI, Japan International Cooperation Agency, DfID, and the sector budget, it is expected that the percentage of the rural population served by CHPS zones will increase significantly by 2015. Those who do not have access to CHPS will continue to access malaria treatment through visiting higher-level public health facilities and private sector vendors. For that reason, PMI will build upon previous years' achievements in providing case management training to health providers in GHS clinics and hospitals, ensuring that supportive supervisory systems are in place to promote quality improvement and adherence to protocols.

The 2011 MICS found that 48.4% of children presenting with fever were not brought for treatment, 3.1% were brought to a CHPS provider, 5.5% were brought to a private sector provider, and 22.8% were brought to a public sector clinic or health center. By improving and expanding the CHPS program, GHS and PMI plans to effect a decrease in the proportion not seeking treatment by shifting a portion of that 48.4% into the category of children who receive appropriate treatment at the peripheral (CHPS) level. PMI expects that the proportion of children receiving care at clinics or hospitals should remain the same or increase and that they will receive better quality of care as a result of PMI technical assistance to those facilities.

The NMCP in Ghana will continue to explore options to scale up diagnosis and treatment of malaria through LCS through pilot programs and Global Fund Phase 2 negotiations. In addition, PMI will provide the NMCP support to explore policy options for RDT roll out and continue to support case management through the private sector LCS. The Pharmacy Council will be used to provide supportive supervision to LCS to improve their dispensing practices and data reporting. This activity will also support pharmacies and LCS to become certified to receive NHIA reimbursement for malaria diagnosis and treatment. LCS serve as the first point of call for many people in the community and underserved areas. A recent study indicated that for 47% of the population LCS was the priority source of malaria treatment. The recent MICS however indicated that only 5.5% of children under five with fever were sent to an LCS compared to 48% that went to a public health facility. Anecdotal information suggests that some of the people who visit public facilities also go to LCS for their medication. Several studies have also highlighted the varied quality of services rendered by the LCS. PMI's SHOPS project works to strengthen the ability of LCS to provide correct information on malaria prevention and appropriate dispensing practices for malaria treatment and to practice appropriate referral practices. SHOPS will work with LCS in five to seven regions. LCS will also be supported to be accredited with the NHIA, so that enrolled clients can easily have their prescriptions served without any out-of-pocket expense.

Improving LCS case management is conducted in partnership with Ghana's Pharmacy Council. In FY 2013, the implementing partner (SHOPS) and the Council developed a training module for LCS on good dispensing practices for malaria. They are currently (July 2013) training LCS in four regions (to be expanded to up to seven) as a component of this year's Continuous Professional Development program, which is administered by Pharmacy Council and is a pre-requisite for re-licensure. Once the training has been completed, interactive sessions will be conducted at the LCS associations monthly meetings at the district level to reinforce the lessons learned.

The Global Fund Phase 2 grant will provide for a continued provision of ACTs for the private sector LCS. There are pilots currently underway funded by the Global Fund evaluating the introduction of RDTs in the private sector. PMI funding will be instrumental in ensuring that LCS are managing malaria cases appropriately and will support RDT introduction when the results of the pilot are known.

PMI will continue to provide funding for ACT procurement, and rectal artesunate for severe malaria as needed. Based on the gap analysis, PMI will prioritize ACT procurements on WHO prequalified pediatric treatments given that the Global Fund is anticipated to provide some support for ACTs in the private sector and that NHIA will continue to reimburse health facilities who supply adult ACT treatments through their own budgets. It is important to note that this gap analysis only covers needs for the public sector.

Table E. ACT Gap Analysis

	2013	2014	2015
National Public Sector Requirement	13,400,000	12,300,000	12,300,000
Global Fund/Other Funders	6,062,194 (estimated)	6,062,194 (estimated)	Unknown
PMI[1]	2,639,440 (actual procured to date)	5,000,000 (pediatric est.)	7,800,000 (pediatric and others est.)
(Gap[2])	(4,698,366)	(1,237,806)	(4,500,000)

[1] The number of RDTs procured in any given year will be driven by actual consumption and need. PMI funded procurement deliveries will be timed accordingly across all three years.
[2] At the time of this writing, the quantification for ACTs was under development and the funding from Global Fund was under negotiation. PMI will adjust deliveries of ACTs, prioritizing pediatric treatments, as needed to fill gaps and alleviate supply concerns to the extent possible.

Since 2012, there have been renewed discussions with the Ghana NHIA on improving the quality of care and financial viability of the insurance scheme. The NHIA is committed to supporting the malaria diagnostic policy and is considering policy options to link reimbursement for malaria treatment to a confirmed parasitological diagnosis. PMI will continue providing support to NHIA to support compliance with the policy, but also to ensure that the reimbursement policy creates incentives for appropriate case management and does "no harm," particularly given that stockouts of RDTs have been common (see Health Systems Strengthening section). Financial incentives for over-diagnosis of malaria should be reviewed, such as paying less for a diagnosis of undifferentiated "febrile illness," even when a parasitological test is negative.

PMI will provide support for pre-service training and BCC activities to address the issues of provider compliance and confidence in malaria RDTs and improve treatment seeking behavior, including demand for diagnostics. In addition, PMI will continue to support pre-service training and continuing medical education through the medical schools and physicians' association on diagnosis and malaria treatment in order to address the ongoing concerns on physician reluctance to abide by the new malaria case management policy. Lack of physician confidence in the new diagnostic policy is impacting lower-level cadres of health professionals from implementing the case management guidance, as the physicians who serve in leadership positions (District Medical Officers, Regional Medical Officers, and Chief Medical Officers) set and influence case management protocols for lower-level clinicians.

Proposed activities with FY 2014 funding ($9,455,000)

- Procure ACTs, SP and severe malaria medication: ($6,700,000)
  PMI will support the procurement of first-line ACTs, with a heavy emphasis on pediatric presentations of ACTs, and SP and severe malaria medication as needed.

- Support to pre-service training for nurses, midwives, and medical assistants: ($265,000)
  PMI will continue to support pre-service training for nurses, midwives, and medical assistants to improve competencies in knowledge, skills, and practices for malaria diagnosis and case management guidelines and treatment protocols. Extend training in

the 28 schools currently supported and increase the number of midwifery and general nursing schools supported to 58 schools.

- Support to Continuing Medical Education and pre-service training for physicians: ($290,000)
  PMI will support pre-service training for medical students and the revision of the medical school curricula to support the new case management guidelines. PMI will also support Continuing Medical Education for accredited practicing physicians through the medical schools and physician associations. Pre-service training for physicians will cover three universities with medical colleges and a fourth school with a medical school only. The colleges encompass medical school, nursing, pharmacy, and lab technology. The implementing partner will conduct a needs assessment, curriculum development, and training and updates for lecturers. The implementing partner will also support the individual professional bodies such as the Pharmaceutical Society and the Medical Association and Nurses and Midwives Council, in their efforts to provide continuous medical education for their members.

- Support improved malaria case management at health facilities: ($1,500,000)
  PMI will collaborate with GHS at all levels to improve compliance with national guidelines for the management of both uncomplicated and severe malaria in health facilities. PMI will provide technical assistance and financial support for supportive supervision, on-the job and class room training, and quality improvement among health workers, with an emphasis on CHPS staff. PMI will support training, supervision, and other measures to link diagnosis to treatment, including promotion of provider adherence to test results. The funding will be allocated between a direct G2G agreement with the GHS (to fund regional and district-level activities) and agreements with two technical assistance partners to ensure nationwide coverage. The implementing partners will conduct at least 2 rounds of supportive supervision in at least 80% of all district and regional facilities with emphasis on CHPS compounds. The projects will provide training for all staff at CHPS compounds that have not been trained in case management and MIP (approximately 90%).

- Support to improved case management through LCS: ($400,000)
  PMI will support activities to build LCS capacity for and compliance with GHS malaria diagnosis, treatment and referral guidelines; address issues related to for-profit, business motivations to comply with GHS guidelines; and support LCS to achieve NHIA accreditation, with emphasis on the geographic areas with gaps in NHIS coverage.

- BCC to improve treatment seeking behavior: ($300,000)
  PMI will support community mobilization and improved demand for case management by targeting the general public to promote correct and consistent use of ACTs. Activities will be integrated with MCH activities as appropriate and will promote community awareness of appropriate testing and treatment. The importance of testing to assess for non-malarial causes of fever will be given special emphasis in urban areas.

CAPACITY BUILDING AND HEALTH SYSTEMS STRENGTHENING

NMCP/PMI Objectives

Although much progress has been made, the MOH continues to have significant gaps in its capacity for program management, commodity and supply chain management, and M&E. By far, the greatest health systems priority for PMI is to strengthen procurement and supply chain management, while also building capacity for quality assurance and supportive supervision and working towards sustainable and equitable health systems.

Progress During the Last 12 Months

PMI has supported capacity building and systems strengthening to improve nursing schools' curricula, practical skills, and teaching skills around malaria. PMI has also piloted routine LLIN distribution systems, supported capacity building of in-service health providers, and improved systems for data collection and analysis.

In the last 12 months, PMI's investments in supply chain and pharmaceutical management have primarily focused on building NMCP capacity to better manage malaria commodities through participation in quantification training, integrated supportive supervision, improvements to the logistics management information system, and end use verification. National quantification exercises for malaria RDTs, ACTs, and severe malaria medicines have been undertaken for the public health facilities and the iCCM program. In addition, PMI investments have been supporting the MOH's development of a Supply Chain Master Plan to address overall public sector supply challenges.

PMI continued to support the Food and Drug Authority (FDA) to monitor the quality of antimalarial drugs, resulting in the testing of 370 antimalarial and analgesic samples from 5 therapeutic efficacy surveillance (TES) sites. Out of the total tested through minilabs or confirmatory testing, 7.7% of antimalarials and 19.8% of analgesics failed. One antimalarial sampled was found to be counterfeit, and almost 9% of antimalarial samples were monotherapy medicines, even though the sale of monotherapies has been banned by the FDA for more than 5 years. Almost 40% of the monotherapies tested were substandard. Although the samples are not nationally representative, the overall 7.7% failure rate of antimalarials is an increase from the previous year's 6.3%. This is the first time since PMI began supporting the FDA that the failure rate increased. Based on these results, the FDA has been recalling substandard and counterfeit products from the market. In mid-2013, the testing program expanded to seven TES sites with PMI support.

During the last year, PMI carried out training for FDA laboratory staff, supported the revision of the FDA laboratory's standard operating procedures, and provided technical assistance to the FDA on WHO Prequalification standards.

PMI, in concert with USAID health programs, supports an integrated health services project which is building the capacity of GHS regional and district health staff to improve program planning, quality of service delivery, and financial management capacity. This has been instrumental in developing regional capacity to manage USG funds directly. In addition to this integrated systems strengthening work, PMI projects have provided sub-agreements to Ghana's regional health management teams to fund supportive supervision for malaria case management. In concert with direct financial and technical support, PMI projects also supported regions to manage resources, report on accomplishments, and submit auditable financial reports. In FY 2014, pending successful implementation with prior year funding, PMI will continue to build on these efforts by directly funding the regions to conduct quality assurance and supportive supervision (see MOP section on case management).

PMI support to the NMCP has included embedding a senior M&E advisor and a senior logistician within the NMCP for two years. Both advisors are supporting activities and providing capacity building in their areas of expertise to the NMCP staff. PMI has supported the School of Public Health at the University of Ghana to establish a "malaria track" within the existing FELTP program. Two GHS staff will continue in their advanced classroom and practical training in field epidemiology, focusing on priority issues in malaria surveillance and operations research identified by the NMCP and PMI.

During the last twelve months, PMI has worked with the NHIA to build the capacity of private sector providers in under-served areas of Ashanti, Brong Ahafo, Central, and Western regions to access financing and information on standards of quality for malaria services. Working closely with the NHIA, PMI is providing LCS in rural areas with training on becoming accredited with the NHIS, which will increase access to malaria diagnosis and treatment. PMI supported the development of guidelines to establish alternative NHIS financing for these small-scale private sector providers.

Challenges, Opportunities, and Threats

The regional and district health teams that have demonstrated capacity to directly manage agreements present an excellent opportunity to use the GHS structure and support Regional Health Management Teams to tailor activities to their specific needs. PMI will provide direct financial support through GHS provided that prior year funding and activities are successfully implemented.

Reform of the health commodity supply chain, while essential to the achievements of PMI goals, is a highly controversial topic. Progress is often slowed by various stakeholders seeking to protect vested interests. While the USG and the Global Fund have intervened at the very highest levels of the GOG to push for these reforms, political will is still tenuous.

NHIA reforms are required over the long term in order to promote the use of diagnostics and appropriate treatment. The NHIA discussions with USAID have continued over the past year; however, certain activities such as the support to clinical audits and policy reforms have been delayed. Therefore, proposed PMI funding for NHIA support in FY 2014 will be at a lower level and focused on targeted technical assistance.

Plans and Justifications

Building upon previous years' accomplishments in building GHS capacity and pending successful implementation in 2013, PMI will continue to directly fund GHS to implement regional quality assurance programs to improve malaria case management (see Treatment section). Regions will be given technical assistance to analyze their specific conditions, confirm malaria cases, assess progress towards achieving malaria control targets, and tailor their activities to address their specific needs. PMI will continue to support the NMCP with an embedded logistics expert and other capacity building within the NMCP staff, including entomology training and limited support for international and/or regional technical meetings. PMI will also support GHS staff to participate in the FELTP training.

PMI will continue to support pharmaceutical management strengthening activities in the areas of quantification, supervision, and end use verification. Due to lack of progress over a decade of investment, PMI has decided to limit its investment in Logistics Management Information Systems. PMI will continue to co-fund the implementation and roll out of the Supply Chain Master Plan to ensure that PMI financed ACTs and RDTs are distributed and managed appropriately.

PMI will provide support to the FDA and drug quality monitoring TES sites. The role of the FDA in ensuring safe, high quality antimalarials will be critically important as current reforms through the Supply Chain Master Plan and NHIA take effect over the next few years. Through enhanced health diplomacy efforts, the USG in Ghana will vigorously promote an increased role for the FDA, increased enforcement, as well as implementation of the Supply Chain Master Plan.

While Ghana has a robust NGO sector in health, most health NGOs have primarily been focused on delivering services. At the same time, rights-based NGOs in Ghana have experience in promoting increasing government accountability and responsiveness. They have been successful advocating for increased legal protection of people with disabilities, for example. USAID Ghana is setting up a new project devoted to increasing capacity to increase effective participation by local NGOs and civil society organizations (CSOs) in monitoring the quality and ease of access to health services and in advocating for improved health care systems and patient's rights. Resources are expected to be sourced from USAID programs in HIV, Family Planning, and MCH, among others. PMI will leverage this project to ensure the inclusion of a strong component of malaria advocacy, with the focus on improved malaria diagnostics and treatment at the facility level. This will include helping NGOs and CSOs to inform and sensitize health care clients and providers about the policies and requirements that govern the health sector, including best practices for malaria case management and the expectation of malaria commodities being present at facilities. PMI and USAID will also support NGOs and CSO in monitoring and holding accountable the performance of district NHIS because it is a critical source of funding for health care for many families.

The NHIS, launched in 2006, has proven its ability to increase mass access to health care services, and PMI will continue to engage with it to improve access to important interventions. Due to delays in launching NHIA activities in the past year, the FY 2014 funding for NHIA will be at a lower level and support targeted technical assistance to assist rural facilities with accreditation to the NHIS, assist providers and patients to ensure continued care as enrollment systems switch over to preferred providers systems, and encourage the general population to seek care at NHIA accredited facilities when they develop malaria symptoms. Similar support will be provided by USAID programs in Family Planning, HIV, and MCH.

Proposed activities with FY 2014 funding ($1,400,000)

- Strengthen logistics and supply chain systems: ($550,000)
  Provide technical assistance for strengthening logistics/supply chain to improve availability of malaria commodities including SP, RDTs, and other commodities. Activities will focus on addressing bottlenecks in finance, management, forecasting, transportation, and reporting systems. Support end use verification activities. Implement Supply Chain Master Plan to reform health commodity procurement and supply.

- Strengthen drug quality monitoring capacity: ($200,000)
  Support the further strengthening of drug quality monitoring in collaboration with the Ghana FDA. Support the recent expansion of the post-market surveillance program (increased frequency and increased number of TES sites). Support increased enforcement capacity, as well as educational efforts to heighten responsiveness to counterfeit and substandard anti-malaria medicines.

- Strengthen management capacity of the NMCP: ($100,000)
  Continue to provide support to the NMCP, GHS, and GOG for technical capacity building and improved malaria control systems. Support limited IT investments to enhance malaria program management.

- Long-term field epidemiology and laboratory training (FELTP): ($150,000)
  Support long-term training of individuals to build capacity at the NMCP or GHS in epidemiology, M&E, or other malaria program management functions as needed. This would be implemented through CDC's FELTP, which was established with USG support at GHS in collaboration with the University of Ghana's School of Public Health.

- Access treatment through National Health Insurance: ($200,000)
  Provide technical assistance to ensure mass access to appropriate malaria treatment through Ghana's NHIS. Promote active enrollment in NHIS and access to NHIS-accredited facilities among the general population, with a focus on high burden rural areas. With MCH and Reproductive Health funds, USAID will directly support the NHIA to accredit new providers in underserved rural areas and conduct clinical audits on their performance. PMI will support this endeavor through the SHOPS program. Support appropriate management of the preferred provider and capitated payment plans in order to ensure continuous access to malaria services by affected regions. With the introduction of a preferred provider system in 2014, incentives for health providers will be reversed, and there is a great risk that patients will be denied appropriate case management services. The NHIA is in need of ongoing technical advice and assistance as they work to introduce the preferred provider model and eventually scale up capitation. With malaria, MCH, and Reproductive Health funds, USAID will provide that technical assistance to the NHIA through the Health Financing and Governance project, providing examples of best practices, analyses of data as it's made available, and communication materials aimed at high-level stakeholders on the topic. The "Systems for Health" project will also work to build understanding and capacity among providers and local schemes on managing a preferred provider payment system.

- Build local civil society capacity for monitoring malaria service provision: ($200,000) Build the capacity of local Ghanaian NGOs and CSOs to monitor the quality and ease of access to health services, with a focus on malaria diagnostics and treatment. Strengthen community structures for advocating for patients' rights and client-centered care, including the availability of malaria commodities. The activity will train and support local NGOs and CSOs in monitoring health services and advocating for improved services as warranted, with a focus on supporting government, community, and service provider dialogues to improve the quality and responsiveness of health services and promote a customer service orientation among health providers. Emphasis will be placed on civil society involvement in monitoring access to quality ACTs and diagnostics.

BEHAVIOR CHANGE COMMUNICATION (BCC)

PMI/NMCP Objectives

The National Malaria Behavior Change Communication Strategy was created by the NMCP with support from PMI's Behavior Change Support project in 2010. The plan provides strategic directions to guide the development, implementation, and monitoring of the communication and behavior change component of malaria prevention and control. It provides a planning framework aimed at defining communication and behavior change objectives, key target groups, messages, channels, and communication interventions at different levels. It revolves around awareness raising about malaria and addressing the key determinants of behavior for prevention and control interventions, with the ultimate goal of a long-term normative shift in malaria related behaviors among the key target groups nationwide. The National Malaria Communication Committee is the body charged with oversight the implementation of the strategy. Officially a sub-committee under the Roll Back Malaria coordination committee, it is a working group with responsibility for reviewing, approving, and initiating the development of communications materials for malaria.

According to the Strategic Plan for Malaria Control 2008 – 2015, priority BCC strategy objectives include: 1) increasing household ownership of LLINs to 90% of households, 2) increasing nightly utilization of LLINs to 85% among children under five years and pregnant women and to 80% among the general population, 3) increasing the percentage of children under five years of age with fever receiving an appropriate ACT within 24 hours of onset of fever and of all patients with uncomplicated malaria correctly managed at public and private health facilities using ACTs to 90%, 4) increasing to 90% caretakers and parents able to recognize early symptoms and signs of malaria, 5) reducing by 50% the proportion of the population that has common misconceptions about causes of malaria, 6) increasing the percent of service providers who promote LLIN, SP and ACTs to clients to 90%, and 7) increasing percent of pregnant women who attend ANC during the first four months of pregnancy and receive their first dose of IPTp after quickening to 90%.

PMI BCC and community mobilization strategy aims to complement the NMCP's effort to promote positive behaviors that support malaria control as defined in the NMCP National Malaria Behavior Change Communication Strategy (2010 – 2015) objectives.

Progress Since PMI Began

PMI was a key partner in the revision of the NMCP National Malaria Behavior Change Communication Strategy (2010 – 2015), which provided the framework upon which all malaria communication activities are implemented. PMI has also continued to support mass media activities, the development of BCC materials, and training of community volunteers in malaria prevention and control in over 1,500 communities. Specialized BCC campaigns have been developed which have focused on specific malaria campaigns, such as universal coverage and related "hang up' campaigns, designed to increase uptake of key behaviors. BCC has been implemented as a cross-cutting activity across all PMI-supported intervention areas. It has been used to target health workers and the general public in the promotion of correct and consistent use of ACTs, promote early presentation at ANC to increase full adherence to IPTp and decrease IRS refusal rates.

With Ghana's relatively well developed media infrastructure, which has grown from five television stations in 2010 to 13 in 2013, viewership and listenership of television and radio continue to increase significantly. According to the 2011 MICS, 56% of women and 63% of men watch television at least once per week and 68.6% of women and 85% men listen to radio at least once per week.

Progress During the Last 12 Months

In the last 12 months, PMI developed additional media spots to elevate awareness about serious complications related to severe malaria infections (e.g. anemia, child development, and brain damage from cerebral malaria), to dispel misconceptions, and to empower people to use ITNs and IPTp by portraying them as positive social norms that are part of a modern lifestyle.

In 2013, 19 community radio stations in 6 regions aired community radio talk programs, jingles, announcements and Live Presenter Mentions on continuous net distribution through schools. Six community radio stations in Eastern and Volta Regions aired jingles, public service announcements, Live Presenter Mentions and radio talk shows on continuous net distribution, and care, maintenance, and proper LLIN use.

Additionally, 72,000 copies of malaria communication materials (*Briefs for Discussion*) were developed and distributed in schools and health facilities, and 96,000 copies of "hang up and care" posters were developed and printed for both schools and health facilities. In addition to open ended scripts, 10,000 malaria flip charts were produced to aid interpersonal communication in schools and communities. Community mobilization has been closely linked with BCC messaging to promote LLIN use, regular ANC attendance and IPTp uptake, and early diagnosis and treatment with ACTs. An estimated 1,524 community volunteers, 50 GHS District Malaria Focal Persons and 100 local NGO staff were trained on various aspects of community mobilization for malaria prevention and control. School staff, ANC staff, and community health workers were all oriented on BCC for the continuous distribution pilot in Eastern Region.

Recognition of PMI-supported malaria messaging was also well captured in the recent 2011 MICS. About half of women and men reported seeing the PMI supported adverts "where a woman doesn't want to stay the night with the man unless he has a treated net" and 42% of women and men reported seeing the short documentaries about the effects of severe malaria on television. A third of the respondents (34%) reported that they saw the music video by a popular artist (called *"Aha ye de"*) and the "advert where people from all walks of life sleep under a treated net"—all PMI supported communication adverts. A smaller percentage of women and men reported hearing the same messages on the radio. This is likely due to the plethora of radio stations that exist in Ghana and suggests that television is a more effective vehicle.

A recent Omnibus Survey in August 2012 further indicated that individuals with higher levels of exposure to the *Aha Ye De* campaign were more likely to own a net, than those with low exposure. Over 60% of women with high exposure reported household LLIN ownership as compared to 48% of women with low exposure.

Challenges, Opportunities, and Threats

While awareness about malaria transmission has increased, many misconceptions persist. Common misconceptions about the cause of malaria identified in the 2011 MICS survey include dirty surroundings (55%), eating contaminated foods (19%), and working in the sun (12%). In the 2011 MICS survey, more respondents identified keeping your surroundings clean (60%) as a means of preventing malaria than those who identified sleeping under an ITN (53%). Additionally, "being too hot/uncomfortable" was the major reason for non-use of nets in a Behavior Change Support Project baseline survey in 2010. It has also been reported that, in some parts of the country (e.g. Northern Region) significant amounts of outdoor sleeping occurs, undermining the effectiveness of malaria prevention efforts.

Moreover, among the general population, the word malaria is often used synonymously with fever, and high rates of presumptive diagnosis of malaria based on fever contribute to the confusion that all or most febrile illness is malaria. In Ghana about 40% of all cases of febrile illness suspected to be malaria are treated at home, and treatment seeking behavior for children needs to be improved. LCS are an important source of malaria treatment; however, most pharmacies and almost all chemical shops stock unapproved antimalarials.

Continued opportunities exist due to Ghana's relatively well-developed media infrastructure and private sector communication agencies. There are 13 television stations, 1 of which has a national reach. Over 100 local radio stations are distributed throughout the country and can be found in almost all districts, with heavier concentrations in the urbanized areas. Local radio stations broadcast in the range of local languages providing opportunities for targeted communications. However, most local stations broadcast over a limited geographic area, and thus, reaching national coverage through radio requires agreements with many different stations. The print media is not as well developed, and only a few news publications are national in character.

Plans and Justification

Following the mass LLIN distribution and hang-up campaigns that have covered almost the entire population of the country, there is an urgent need to follow up with BCC messages to:

- o increase threat perception (e.g. Malaria being #1 killer for children under five, severe malaria causes disability),
- o increase knowledge about how malaria carrying mosquitos bite at night and how LLINs provide protection, signs and symptoms of malaria, and proper care seeking behaviors, and
- o facilitate adjustment in attitudes and social norms in a way that LLINs become a lifestyle product that are used consistently and swift care seeking behavior becomes the norm in case of febrile illness.

USAID/Ghana will be building on previous investments in BCC and branding of the Goodlife health messaging campaign that was used to support malaria BCC. PMI will continue to support dissemination and implementation of community mobilization and communications activities and materials (print and mass media) to:

- o promote LLIN ownership and regular use for prevention of malaria, including malaria specific BCC and incorporating LLIN messages into national health promotion BCC efforts,
- o increase prompt and appropriate care seeking behavior for malaria symptoms (e.g. clinic attendance at first sign of fever, particularly for children under five years old and pregnant women) and correct and complete use of ACTs,
- o increase the use of RDTs for confirmation of suspected malaria cases,
- o promote ACTs as the drug of choice for treatment of malaria,
- o improve administration of IPTp by healthcare workers,
- o promote IPTp with particular focus on geographic areas and/or cultural groups with low IPTp rates,
- o integrate malaria-related BCC messages with MCH BCC activities as appropriate, and
- o provide technical assistance to the NMCP and the National Malaria Communications Committee.

As PMI scales up improved case management and IPTp, it will integrate community-level BCC messaging to strengthen the role of health workers as active promoters of LLINs, IPTp, and ACTs.

PMI will continue to disseminate and leverage the existing branded BCC communications materials and revise as appropriate. The effectiveness of BCC activities will be assessed through questions and analysis of the 2014 DHS or Malaria Indicator Survey. Local media monitoring organizations will be used to monitor the number of spots aired on radio and television.

Proposed activities with FY 2014 funding (Funding levels indicated in each technical section)

- BCC and community mobilization to promote LLIN ownership and use: (See LLIN Section)
  PMI will support the dissemination and implementation of community mobilization and communications activities to promote LLIN ownership and use. Particular focus will be placed on net care and misperceptions about use. Technical assistance will be provided to the NMCP and the National Malaria Communications Committee.

- BCC to promote IPTp: (See IPTp Section)
  PMI will support the distribution and use of communications materials to improve administration of IPTp by healthcare workers and will support community mobilization and communications materials (print and mass media) to promote IPTp with a particular focus on geographic areas with low IPTp rates. Messages will be integrated with MCH BCC activities as appropriate.

- BCC to improve malaria-related care/treatment seeking behavior: (See Treatment Section)
  PMI will support community mobilization and mass communication to improve demand will be used to increase prompt and appropriate care seeking behavior for malaria symptoms. Communications activities will target the general public to promote correct and consistent use of ACTs and confirmatory testing. The importance of testing to assess for non-malarial causes of fever will be given special emphasis in urban areas. Activities will be integrated with MCH activities as appropriate.

Though the activities described above are captured under different sections of the MOP, during implementation these activities will be integrated for maximal cost and time savings, rather than implementing each one separately.

MONITORING AND EVALUATION

NMCP/PMI Objectives

The *National Malaria Control Monitoring and Evaluation Plan (2008-2015)* guides the strategic framework for M&E in malaria control in Ghana. The plan was developed in conjunction with the revised national strategic plan by the NMCP with technical assistance from PMI, WHO, and other partners.

In accordance with the national M&E plan, the Policy, Planning, and M&E Division within GHS, was built using structures already in place to improve and strengthen the routine data systems. The GHS collaborated with the University of Oslo to upgrade Ghana's DHIMS by placing it on the platform of the web-based, internationally recommended "District Health Information System" software. The new system, called DHIMS2, is a comprehensive health information management system for reporting and analyzing district level data from health facilities. The DHIMS2 came online in April 2012 and is currently available in all 216 districts.

PMI provided support towards the DHIMS2 upgrade, which now includes a customized dashboard to collect malaria-focused indicators. The NMCP eventually expects to rely on the DHIMS2 data for its reporting, analysis, and programmatic decisions. However, since the system is still fairly new, gaps in the completeness and accuracy of the data have been observed, necessitating a comprehensive evaluation of DHMIS2 data management procedures. PMI's objective is to help increase the completeness and ensure accuracy of the health facility malaria data in DHIMS2 so that the NMCP can provide reliable reports and inform programmatic decisions on all facility-based malaria indicators.

Since 2008, PMI has supported two national malaria household surveys, the DHS 2008 and the MICS 2011. Both were conducted during the peak malaria season--late rainy season from August to December. The 2008 DHS serves as the baseline estimate for all PMI coverage indicators and includes a malaria module comprised of anemia testing, verbal autopsy evaluations, intervention coverage indicators, and knowledge/attitude/practice indicators.

PMI and the NMCP provided financial support and technical assistance for the inclusion of malaria biomarkers in the 2011 MICS: anemia testing and malaria testing using RDTs and microscopy. This cross-sectional, nationally representative household survey was implemented under the overall leadership of the Ghana Statistical Service and UNICEF. Results showed that anemia prevalence (Hb<8.0 g/dL) ranged from 2% in the Eastern Region to 19% in the Northern Region among children aged 6-59 months. Malaria prevalence, as determined by microscopy, was 28% in children age 6-59 months and increased steadily from 16% among those 6-8 months of age to 34% among those 48-59 months. All-cause, under-five mortality was 82 deaths per 1,000 live births for the five-year period preceding the MICS.

Progress During the Last 12 Months

To improve M&E capacity-building within the NMCP, PMI has supported an M&E Advisor seconded to the NMCP since 2011. This enhanced efficiency in NMCP data reporting, provided in-house mentoring for the NMCP's M&E staff, and provided technical leadership for the malaria surveys. PMI also provided support for laptops, desktop computers, and printers to improve data management and analysis. Additionally, two FELTP candidates completed a malaria-track, which was established in 2011 (as described under the Capacity Building/Health Systems Strengthening section).

Accurate and timely data collection is one of the NMCP's most immediate challenges. During the last 12 months, PMI continued to work with the NMCP and other partners to improve the quality of data and build capacity for evidence-based decision making. Support was at the national, regional and district/sub-district levels and included:

- Printing an additional 8,000 copies of the revised consulting room registers for distribution to 2,700 health facilities in 126 districts within 7 regions. These registers were designed with PMI assistance to help facilities readily capture malaria diagnoses as provisional versus confirmed cases.
- Supporting regional Health Information Officers in 3 regions to train 610 health workers in using the consulting room register.

- Providing 48 computers at the district level to help strengthen data management.
- Supporting supervisory visits to conduct data quality assessments and coaching at 132 health facilities in 4 regions.
- Training, in collaboration with the Policy, Planning and M&E Division, 60 Health Information Officers from all 10 regions on the use of DHIMS2 data to generate malaria bulletins.
- Supporting seven quarterly reviews of malaria data at the regional level.

In collaboration with NMCP/GHS and the University of Ghana School of Public Health, PMI conducted The Ghana Urban Malaria Study. Using the triangulation method, the study sought to identify: 1) the evidence that the burden of malaria is lower in urban areas than in rural areas; 2) the most important determinants of the burden of malaria within urban areas; 3) how coverage with malaria control interventions differ between urban and rural areas; and 4) some important determinants of the coverage of urban areas with malaria control interventions. A team of analysts compiled data from 19 available research studies, 4 large household survey datasets and all data reported by health facilities to the GHS each month since January 2011 on outpatient malaria morbidity and malaria testing. Their analysis showed that 1) children living in the large urban areas of Accra, Kumasi and Tamale had a significantly lower risk of being malaria-infected compared to children living in rural areas within the same ecological zone, 2) 80% of rural-area children reporting fever in the previous 2 weeks tested positive for malaria, compared to less than 7% for those children living in Accra and Kumasi, with rural and urban children receiving the same benefit from malaria control practices, 3) a high level of presumptive diagnosis in Accra, with 11% of children with fever having a positive microscopy, but 80% being diagnosed with malaria, and 4) data on routinely reported malaria testing are often incomplete and inconsistent – resulting in an unreliable indication of the burden of malaria in Ghana. The results from this study provide quantifiable evidence for developing malaria control recommendations that are demographically and geographically appropriate, compared to a "one size fits all" strategy. It also reinforces the need for health professionals to perform malaria test on all suspected cases and to adhere to current practices and guidelines for diagnosis and treatment of confirmed malaria cases.

The high levels of ITN coverage and the growing use of IRS underscore the need to measure and manage insecticide resistance in *Anopheles* mosquito vectors throughout Ghana. In support of this goal, PMI provided technical assistance to Malaria Vector Control Oversight Committee to develop a concept paper for the national insecticide resistance monitoring plan. The secretariat will be housed at the Noguchi Institute. Data generated by existing IRS programs (such as Global Fund, PMI, mines) will be collated and harmonized; in addition, standardized monitoring and reporting will be carried out at up to twenty sites in each of the ten regions, to fill gaps, directed by the NMCP via regional biologists. Noguchi and the IRS project are now working to operationalize the plan.

There are currently ten Global Fund-supported TES sites, operated by Noguchi Institute, for *in vivo* drug efficacy monitoring throughout Ghana. PMI, WHO, and Naval Medical Research Unit/Department of Defense have also provided support for drug efficacy monitoring, although coordination and data sharing has proven difficult. The program calculates the par-correction Adequate Clinical and Parasitological Response rates. In 2012, Noguchi released a report on monitoring in 2010-11, which suggested that the 2 first-line ACTS used for the treatment of uncomplicated malaria remain therapeutically effective, with failure rates of less than 4%.

Under the Phase II Global Fund grant, the NMCP and Noguchi are developing plans to expand the scope of these TES sites to include malaria surveillance indicators such as test positivity rates; they also aim to increase the number of sites to 26 (4 each in the 3 northern regions, which are of special concern, and 2 each in the remaining 7 regions). The protocol would aim for a robust, practical approach which can be replicated across sites and sustained over time.

Challenges, Opportunities, and Threats

The new, web-based DHIMS2 dramatically increased data visibility. With a much more 'user-friendly' dashboard, the NMCP, regional and district health facilities can generate reports on malaria indicators more rapidly. As a result, Ghana is now able to generate malaria bulletins. Over time, regular publication of these bulletins may prove to be a powerful data feedback mechanism to identify and correct deficiencies at the regional and district levels. However, a key challenge is improving the quality of malaria data entered into DHIMS2, specifically completeness, consistency, and accuracy. Additionally, as more districts implement this health management system, resources to ensure consistent training and operating procedures, supervision, auditing, and troubleshooting are needed.

Using FY 2013 reprogrammed funds and FY 2014 funds, PMI has the opportunity to support a nation-wide routine health information systems (RHIS) strengthening project, which will be an evaluation of the DHIMS2, to improve the quality and use of routine malaria data in collaboration with the Ghana NMCP and its stakeholders. The project will consist of three phases: 1) comprehensive situational analysis and the development of a Ghana-specific RHIS strengthening strategy, 2) implementation of the developed strategy, and 3) evaluation of strategy's implementation (not the final outcomes of this malaria RHIS strengthening project). This project will be NMCP-led, focus on achievable activities that have measureable outcomes, and although malaria-focused, will be part of broader routine health information system activities.

The plans to expand malaria surveillance sites in the country are welcome, but care is needed to develop a sustainable and reliable system. In 2008-2010, PMI had supported 5 GHS sentinel sites, collecting both patient-level and aggregate data on up to 30 malaria indicators. PMI stopped providing financial and technical support, following an evaluation in 2011, which showed that sites in Ghana and other countries were not meeting their target testing rates and were largely not generating useful data. Since there still remains a need for high-quality facility-based longitudinal malaria data, the NMCP has expressed interest in adding more sites, using a new simpler, yet more robust methodology. In collaboration with the M&E Workgroup, PMI will only provide technical assistance in establishing surveillance protocols for the sentinel sites. PMI, using best practices from other countries and domestically, may help the NMCP develop new models for malaria surveillance. These new models might include selecting high-performing sites that are easily accessible or using temporary staff augmentation at the facility to obtain high-quality laboratory confirmed malaria case numbers.

Due to unforeseen administrative and funding issues, the DHS planned for the 2013 rainy season was postponed and is planned for August, 2014. Using FY 2013 reprogrammed funds, PMI will support the 2014 DHS, which will include parasitemia biomarkers as part of the malaria component.

Results from the 2014 DHS will help inform an evaluation of impact that PMI, together with other partners, is completing on malaria-related illnesses and deaths in Ghana. This impact evaluation was scheduled to take place with FY 2014 funds, but has also been delayed until results from the 2014 DHS are available.

Plans and Justification

PMI support for routine information system strengthening continues to be guided by the findings of a joint PMI-WHO-Roll Back Malaria-GHS mission held in Ghana in 2010 to strengthen the capacity of DHIMS and the system's ability to capture quality malaria data. The mission resulted in a set of recommendations focusing on: 1) improving data quality supervision; 2) improving DHIMS data use and feedback; and 3) improving facility data quality.

PMI is committed to working with the NMCP in the monitoring of the new reporting DHIMS2 and providing technical assistance when necessary. PMI will monitor the quality of malaria data collected through DHIMS2 to ensure that the programmatic needs of NMCP are met; collaborate with NMCP to resolve problems in a timely manner as they are identified; monitor whether DHIMS2 data are being used by the NMCP; and provide necessary training to ensure that data are analyzed and utilized. These activities will be conducted largely through the proposed RHIS strengthening project but will also include PMI/'s continued support for training and supervision of Health Information Officers at data entry sites and integration of DHIMS2 data with OTSS and other facility data

Given the changing epidemiology of the *Anopheles* mosquito, the rotation of insecticides used during spraying, and the shift in spray areas, PMI recognizes the importance of enhanced monitoring of insecticide resistance, and will continue to support this activity in FY 2014.

Under the Global Fund Phase II grant, approximately $1 million is committed to providing funds for M&E activities until the end of calendar year 2014. This funding will support activities that include supervisory visits, data quality reviews and training for DHIMS2 staff. However, since Global Fund has not committed to funding a 2015 *in vivo* drug efficacy study, as in previous years, PMI will provide support to cover the gap and implement the WHO protocol, 'Methods for Surveillance of Antimalarial Drug Efficacy.' Prior to conducting the study, PMI will support the review of previous drug efficacy studies conducted in Ghana to evaluate trends and identify gaps, which will help inform implementation of the 2015 *in vivo* study.

Proposed Activities with FY 2014 funding ($619,000)

- Strengthen and support routine M&E systems: ($415,000)

- o Provide continued support for GHS/NMCP to strengthen routine systems for malaria M&E, including training and supportive supervision of district and regional staff on data collection, reporting and analysis, and providing limited computer hardware and software to fill gaps. Support strengthening the quality of malaria data including scaling-up dissemination of revised patient registers and continued implementation of a robust DHIMS2. Support the production and circulation of regular malaria bulletins using standardized indicators. Encourage the reconvening of an M&E technical working group that will support NMCP to analyze and utilize data from routine systems to inform programmatic decisions.
- o Support the nationwide RHIS strengthening project, which will produce a situational/SWOT (strength, weakness, opportunities, and threats) analysis, based on a desk review, stakeholder input, and field-based data collection – as well as an RHIS strengthening strategy, which will include both a work and M&E plan.

- Nationwide insecticide resistance monitoring: ($50,000)
  In collaboration with other partners and national research institutions, continue to support routine insecticide resistance monitoring at a network of sites nationwide. PMI will provide technical assistance, equipment training, and funding for routine data collection. These resources will leverage other vector-control partner resources for entomological monitoring activities and will help fill gaps to ensure national coverage.

- Drug efficacy monitoring: ($130,000)
  Support *in vivo* efficacy evaluations of first-line antimalarial drugs in three to four TES sites where routine periodic evaluations have been ongoing. Include a review of past efficacy studies in Ghana to assess trends and knowledge gaps. The WHO protocol, 'Methods for Surveillance of Antimalarial Drug Efficacy,' will be followed and studies conducted in calendar year 2015.

- Technical assistance: ($24,000)
  Support for technical assistance from the CDC PMI M&E team. Technical assistance will include working with the NMCP to guide evaluation of the malaria sentinel surveillance systems, continued support for the implementation and evaluation of DHIMS2 at all levels of the system, and support for IRS epidemiologic monitoring.

Table F. Current and projected monitoring and evaluation data sources, 2007 - 2016

Data Source	Year[5]									
	2007	2008	2009	2010	2011	2012	2013	2014	2015	2016
Household Surveys[1]										
Demographic Health Survey		X						X		
Multiple Indicator Cluster Survey (MICS)					X					
Malaria Indicator Survey					X					
Other Surveys[2]										
End-Use Verification Survey				X	X	X				
Anemia and parasitemia monitoring				X	X	X				
Impact evaluation									X	
Drug efficacy monitoring							X		X	
Malaria Surveillance and routine system support[3]										
Sentinel surveillance		X	X	X	X					
Vector resistance surveillance					X	X	X	X	X	
Entomology surveillance		X	X	X	X	X	X	X	X	

[1] All household surveys and the years they were conducted or are planned to be conducted.
[2] All other surveys (national and sub-national), including health facility surveys and EUV. Includes non- or partial PMI funded surveys.
[3] All PMI funded surveillance and routine system support activities, including sentinel surveillance, epidemic detection and response and/or IRS disease monitoring.
[4] Years listed reflect when PMI began in the country

55

STAFFING AND ADMINISTRATION

Two health professionals serve as Resident Advisors to oversee the PMI in Ghana, one representing CDC and one representing USAID. In addition, one or more FSNs work as part of the PMI team. All PMI staff members are part of a single inter-agency team led by the USAID Mission Director or his/her designee in country. The PMI team shares responsibility for development and implementation of PMI strategies and work plans, coordination with national authorities, managing collaborating agencies and supervising day-to-day activities. Candidates for resident advisor positions (whether initial hires or replacements) will be evaluated and/or interviewed jointly by USAID and CDC, and both agencies will be involved in hiring decisions, with the final decision made by the individual agency.

The PMI professional staff work together to oversee all technical and administrative aspects of the PMI, including finalizing details of the project design, implementing malaria prevention and treatment activities, monitoring and evaluation of outcomes and impact, reporting of results, and providing guidance to PMI partners.

The PMI lead in country is the USAID Mission Director. The two PMI resident advisors, one from USAID and one from CDC, report to the Senior USAID Health Officer for day-to-day leadership, and work together as a part of a single interagency team. The technical expertise housed in Atlanta and Washington guides PMI programmatic efforts and thus overall technical guidance for both RAs falls to the PMI staff in Atlanta and Washington. Since CDC resident advisors are CDC employees (CDC USDD—38), responsibility for completing official performance reviews lies with the CDC Country Director who is expected to rely upon input from PMI staff across the two agencies that work closely day in and day out with the CDC RA and thus best positioned to comment on the RA's performance.

The two PMI resident advisors are based within the USAID health office and are expected to spend approximately half their time sitting with and providing technical assistance to the national malaria control programs and partners.

Locally-hired staff to support PMI activities either in Ministries or in USAID will be approved by the USAID Mission Director. Because of the need to adhere to specific country policies and USAID accounting regulations, any transfer of PMI funds directly to Ministries or host governments will need to be approved by the USAID Mission Director and Controller, in addition to the PMI Coordinator.

Table 1: Ghana FY 2014 Budget by Mechanism				
Partner	**Geographical Area**	**Budget ($)**	**% of Total**	**Activity**
DELIVER	**National**	12,350,000	46%	Procure LLINs for routine distribution and mass campaigns; procure antimalarial medications and laboratory equipment; strengthen logistics and supply chain systems
IRS IQC TO4	**Northern Region**	4,570,000	17%	Provide TA, procure pesticides, conduct spraying operations in support of IRS implementation.
MalariaCare	**National**	2,335,000	9%	Strengthen malaria diagnosis, treatment, and support the national M&E strategy; strengthen NGO capacity and support NMCP management and supervision. Support implementation of the malaria laboratory policy, OTSS, Continuing Medical Education/pre-service training for providers
TBD	**National**	650,000	2%	Support malaria BCC activities for all programs focused on vulnerable groups
TBD	**Central, Western and Greater Accra**	565,000	1%	Support pre-service training for general nurses, midwives, and medical assistants. Support implementation of revised school curricula. Develop training for managing cases with negative malaria test results.
TBD	**National**	200,000	6%	Support ITN distributions and promotion
TBD	**National**	1,790,000	7%	Provide technical assistance for supportive supervision, on-the job and class room training, and quality improvement among HCWs, with an emphasis on CHPS. Collaborate with GHS/NMCP to achieve high rates of parasitological testing, with focus on scaling up RDT use in clinical settings, promotion of IPTp uptake. Support strengthening the quality of malaria data.

G2G Activities with GHS for Centrally Managed Activities: $1,420,000 **G2G Agreement with GHS for Regional Activities: $500,000** **G2G Activities with Noguchi: $50,000**	**National**	**1,970,000**	**7%**	Support the continuous distribution of LLINS through schools and health facilities and communications activities to promote ownership and use. Support community mobilization. Support continued quality improvements to malaria microscopy at the laboratory level, building upon and scaling up the successful OTSS program. Focus on implementing supportive supervision and incentivizing health care providers. Support routine insecticide resistance monitoring at a network of sites.
TBD	**National**	**200,000**	**1%**	Build the capacity of local Ghanaian NGOs and CSOs to monitor the quality and ease of access to malaria testing and treatment services. Strengthen community structures for advocating for patients' rights and client-centered care. Emphasize public access to quality ACTs and diagnostics.
U.S. Pharmacopeia	**National**	**200,000**	**1%**	Strengthen drug quality monitoring
Health Financing and Governance	**National**	**200,000**	**1%**	Promote active enrollment in NHIA and access to NHIA-accredited facilities among the general population, with a focus on high burden rural areas.
CDC	**National**	**220,000**	**1%**	Provide technical assistance for microscopy QA and RDT scale up; technical assistance for ento monitoring (includes two entomology visits plus equipment and supplies); support for technical assistance from the CDC PMI M&E team for DHS and routine surveillance systems; FELTP

SHOPS	**National**	**400,000**	**1%**	Support activities to build LCS and pharmacists capacity for and compliance with GHS malaria diagnosis, treatment and referral guidelines. Support LCS to achieve NHIA accreditation, with emphasis on geographic areas with gaps in NHIS coverage.
Admin		**1,350,000**	**5%**	Coordination and management of all in-country PMI activities including staff salaries and benefits. Includes posting of one USAID and one CDC resident advisor to Accra.
Total		**27,000,000**	**100%**	

Table 2: Ghana FY2014 Budget by Activity

ITNs

Proposed Activity	Mechanism	FY 2014	Geographical area	Description
Procure and transport LLINs	DELIVER	1,500,000	National	Procure a minimum of 300,000 LLINs at $5 per LLIN (estimated 8% of national need) to replace expired LLINs and to maintain LLIN universal coverage. Budget includes transportation of LLINs to distribution points.
LLIN distribution and supply chain	DELIVER	300,000	National	Provide technical assistance to GHS, GES, and other stakeholders to strengthen routine LLIN distribution planning, logistics, supply chain management, training, and end-user distribution systems. Second ITN distribution experts to GHS. Conduct assessments of net distribution as appropriate.
	TBD	200,000		
	G2G: GHS and Ghana Education Service	770,000	3 regions	Through G2G mechanism with GHS/NMCP and GES/SHEP, support the continuous distribution of LLINS through schools and health facilities. Fund costs of training, planning, supervision, operations and M&E, on a cost-sharing basis.
BCC and community mobilization to promote LLIN ownership and use	TBD	150,000	National	Support the development and implementation of communications activities to promote LLIN ownership and use, employing an evidence-based approach.. Support community mobilization, radio and television spots, and communications materials. Focus on net care and misperceptions about use. Provide technical assistance to the NMCP and the National Malaria Communications Committee, and SHEP.
	G2G with GHS/NMCP and GES/SHEP	350,000		
SUBTOTAL ITNs		**3,270,000**		

IRS

Proposed Activity	Mechanism	FY 2014	Geographical area	Description
Indoor Residual Spraying	IQC TO4	4,570,000	TBD	In collaboration with GHS, and with continued focus on capacity building, support IRS implementation and programmatic evaluation in targeted districts. Districts will be selected by December 2013 for optimal IRS impact on morbidity. Targeting will be based on the recommendations of the ongoing national Scoping Exercise, as well as epidemiologic and entomologic monitoring data from PMI and AGA/Global Fund IRS programs. Encompasses entomological monitoring and limited epidemiologic monitoring, spray operations, data collection, environmental assessment and compliance monitoring, BCC activities including community mobilization, and logistics support. .
TA to support entomological monitoring for IRS	CDC	34,000	Northern Region and National	Technical assistance and quality assurance for entomologic monitoring, including insecticide resistance management. Budget includes 2 entomology visits plus equipment and supplies.
SUBTOTAL IRS		**4,604,000**		

Malaria in Pregnancy

Proposed Activity	Mechanism	FY 2014	Geographical area	Description
Strengthen ANC services and in-service training	TBD	540,000	Minimum of 5 Regions	Support the GHS to further improve HCW/health system capacity to effectively deliver a package of malaria prevention and care services to pregnant women. PMI support will focus on supportive supervision, on-site training as needed, quality improvement to increase HCW administration of all three IPTp doses, and support for implementing updated GHS guidance.
Support pre-service training	TBD	300,000	National	Provide technical pre-service training for nurses, midwives, and medical assistants in prevention of MIP.
Support BCC to promote IPTp	TBD	200,000	5 Regions	Support the distribution and use of communications materials to improve administration of IPTp by healthcare workers. Support community mobilization and communications materials (print and mass media) to
	TBD	200,000	National	promote IPTp with a particular focus on geographic areas and/or cultural groups with low IPTp rates.
SUBTOTAL MIP		**1,240,000**		

Case Management – Diagnosis

Proposed Activity	Mechanism	FY 2014	Geographical area	Description
Procure RDTs and other lab supplies	DELIVER	3,300,000	National	Procure approximately 5, 250,000 RDTs (approximately $0.60/RDT) to meet 40-50% of national RDT need and to procure limited microscopes and microscopy kits to fill gaps.
Strengthen quality of microscopy and RDT use at Laboratory level	MalariaCare	200,000	National	Support continued quality improvements to malaria microscopy at the laboratory level, building upon and scaling up the successful OTSS program. Provide

62

Proposed Activity	Mechanism		Geographical area	Description
	G2G: GHS CLU	300,000		supportive supervision and on-the-job training of laboratory personnel, complemented by refresher training for lab supervisors. Focus on improving the efficiency of testing processes and on using the test results to inform clinical decisions and surveillance Emphasize the transfer of increased management responsibility to the GHS CLU.
Scale up RDT use in Clinical Settings	TBD	500,000	5 Regions	Collaborate with GHS/NMCP to achieve high rates of parasitological testing, with focus on scaling up RDT use in clinical settings. Accelerate efforts to identify and remove operational, financial and policy barriers to increased RDT use. Support capacity building to ensure consistent availability and use of RDTs at public health facilities, esp. CHPS. Support the roll-out of RDTs to community-based agents, LCS and pharmacies.
	MalariaCare	750,000	National	
TA for diagnostics	CDC	12,000	National	Provide technical assistance for microscopy QA and to realize full potential of RDTs at all levels
SUBTOTAL CM - Diagnosis		**5,062,000**		
Case Management – Treatment				
Proposed Activity	**Mechanism**	**FY 2014**	**Geographical area**	**Description**
Procure malaria medication	DELIVER	6,700,000	National	Procure ACTs in quantities sufficient to cover pediatric ACT requirements. Secondarily, procure adult ACT formulations, rectal artesunate, severe malaria drugs, and SP for IPTp as necessary to fill gaps and prevent stockouts.

Activity	Implementer	Location	Budget	Description
Support pre-service training	TBD	National	265,000	Support pre-service training for general nurses, midwives, and medical assistants to improve competencies in knowledge, skills, and practices for malaria diagnosis and case management in compliance with GHS guidelines and protocols. Support implementation of revised school curricula. Develop training for managing cases with negative malaria test results.
	MalariaCare (physician cadre)	National	290,000	Support pre-service and/or Continuing Medical Education training for physicians and revision of medical school curricula to improve competencies in knowledge, skills, and practices for malaria diagnosis and case management in compliance with GHS guidelines and protocols. Fill gaps in other pre-service training as appropriate.
TA to Improve Malaria Case Management at Health Facilities	G2G	5 regions	500,000	Provide financial support to GHS regional and districts teams to promote improved malaria case management. Focus on implementing supportive supervision and incentivizing health care providers.
	MalariaCare	National level and 5 regions	600,000	Collaborate with GHS to improve compliance with national guidelines for management of uncomplicated and severe malaria in health facilities. Provide technical assistance for supportive supervision, on-the job and class room training, and quality improvement among HCWs, with an emphasis on CHPS staff. Promote provider adherence to test results.
	TBD	5 regions	400,000	
Support Licensed Chemical Sellers & Pharmacies	SHOPS	National	400,000	Support activities to build LCS and pharmacists capacity for and compliance with GHS malaria diagnosis, treatment and referral guidelines. Address issues related to for-profit, business motivations to comply with GHS guidelines. Support LCS to achieve NHIA accreditation, with emphasis on geographic areas with gaps in NHIS coverage.

Proposed Activity	Mechanism	FY 2014	Geographical area	Description
Support BCC to improve malaria-related care/treatment seeking behavior	TBD	300,000	National	Support community mobilization and improved demand for case management to promote correct and consistent use of ACTs and confirmatory testing, targeting the general public. The importance of testing before treating will receive increased emphasis in urban areas. Integrate activities with MCH activities as appropriate. Provide technical assistance to GHS (NMCP, NMCC, and HPU).
SUBTOTAL CM - Treatment		**9,455,000**		
Case Management Subtotal		**14,517,000**		
Capacity Building and Health System Strengthening				
Proposed Activity	**Mechanism**	**FY 2014**	**Geographical area**	**Description**
Strengthen logistics and supply chain systems	DELIVER	550,000	National	Provide technical assistance for strengthening logistics/supply chain to improve availability of malaria commodities including SP, RDTs, and other commodities. Activities will focus on addressing bottlenecks in finance, management, forecasting, transportation and reporting systems. Support end use verification activities. Implement Supply Chain Master Plan to reform health commodity procurement and supply.
Strengthen drug quality monitoring capacity	U.S. Pharmacopeia	200,000	National	Support the strengthening of anti-malaria drug quality monitoring in collaboration with the Ghana FDA. Consolidate the recent expansion of the post-market surveillance Support increased enforcement capacity and education. to heighten responsiveness to counterfeit and substandard medicines.
Build management capacity at NMCP, GHS and other GOG partners	Malariacare	100,000	National	Continue to provide support to the NMCP, GHS, and GOG for technical capacity building and improved malaria control systems. Support limited IT investments to enhance malaria program management.

Proposed Activity	Mechanism		Geographical area	Description
Long term Training – Field Epidemiology and Laboratory Training Program	CDC	150,000	National	Continue to support long term training of two individuals from GHS/NMCP in epidemiology, surveillance, monitoring and evaluation. To be implemented as a "malaria track" imbedded in FELTP program at the U. Ghana.
Assure mass access to appropriate malaria treatment through National Health Insurance	Health Financing & Governance	200,000	National	Provide technical assistance to assure mass access to appropriate malaria treatment through NHIA program. Promote active enrollment in NHIA and access to NHIA-accredited facilities among the general population, with a focus on high burden rural areas.
Strengthen Civil Society Role in Malaria Advocacy	TBD	200,000	National	Build the capacity of local Ghanaian NGOs and CSOs to monitor the quality and ease of access to malaria testing and treatment services. Strengthen community structures for advocating for patients' rights and client-centered care. Emphasize public access to quality ACTs and diagnostics.
SUBTOTAL - Capacity / HSS		**1,400,000**		
Monitoring and Evaluation				
Proposed Activity	**Mechanism**	**FY 2014**	**Geographical area**	**Description**
Strengthen Routine M&E Systems	MalariaCare	265,000	National level and 5 regions	Support GHS/NMCP to strengthen routine systems for malaria M&E, including training district and regional staff on data collection, analysis and reporting; and limited computer hardware and software to fill gaps. Support strengthening the quality of malaria data.. Support GHS and NMCP stakeholders to perform assessment of routinely collected malaria data., assessment and use.

Proposed Activity	Mechanism	FY 2014	Geographical area	Description
	TBD	150,000	5 regions	Support GHS/ at regional level to strengthen routine systems for malaria M&E, including training district and regional staff on data collection, analysis and reporting; and limited computer hardware and software to fill gaps. Support strengthening the quality of malaria data.
National insecticide resistance surveillance	G2G: Noguchi	50,000	National	In collaboration with other partners and research institutions continue to support routine insecticide resistance monitoring at a network of sites.
Drug efficacy monitoring	MalariaCare	130,000	National	Support *in vivo* efficacy evaluations of first-line antimalarial drugs in three to four sites where routine periodic evaluations have been ongoing.
Technical assistance	CDC	24,000	National	Support for technical assistance from the CDC PMI M&E team
SUBTOTAL – M & E		**489,000**		

Staff and Administration

Proposed Activity	Mechanism	FY 2014	Geographical area	Description
In-country staff and administrative expenses	USAID Ghana & CDC IAA	1,350,000		Coordination and management of all in-country PMI activities including staff salaries and benefits. Includes posting of one USAID and one CDC resident advisor to Accra.
SUBTOTAL In-Country Staff		**1,350,000**		
GRAND TOTAL		**27,000,000**		

www.ingramcontent.com/pod-product-compliance
Lightning Source LLC
Chambersburg PA
CBHW080532290526
45790CB00006B/2375